BEST DARN FOOD EVER!

CHICKEN PIZZAIOLA WITH TORN BASIL AND CAPERS, PAGE 137

WeightWatchers®
PointsPlus®

BEST DARN FOOD EVER!

140
Comfort Classics
You CAN Eat
on Plan

KENTUCKY HOT BROWNS,
PAGE 44

ABOUT

WeightWatchers®

Weight Watchers International, Inc. is the world's leading provider of weight-management services, operating globally through a network of company-owned and franchise operations. Weight Watchers holds nearly 50,000 weekly meetings worldwide, at which members receive group support and education about healthful eating patterns, behavior modification, and physical activity. Weight-loss and weight-management results vary by individual. We recommend that you attend Weight Watchers meetings to benefit from the supportive environment you find there and follow the comprehensive Weight Watchers program, which includes a food plan, an activity plan, and a behavioral component. In addition, Weight Watchers offers a wide range of products, publications, and programs for people interested in weight loss and weight control. For the Weight Watchers meeting nearest you, call **1-800-651-6000**. For information about bringing Weight Watchers to your workplace, call **1-800-8AT-WORK**. Also visit us at our Web site, **WeightWatchers.com**, and look for **Weight Watchers Magazine** at your newsstand or in your meeting room.

Weight Watchers Publishing Group

VP, Editorial Director **Nancy Gagliardi**

Creative Director **Ed Melnitsky**

Photo Director **Deborah Hardt**

Managing Editor **Diane Pavia**

Editorial Assistant **Katerina Gkionis**

Food Editor **Eileen Runyan**

Editor **Deborah Mintcheff**

Recipe Developers **Georgia Downard, Lori Longbotham, Maureen Luchejko**

Production Manager **Alan Biederman**

Photographer **David Malosh**

Food Stylist **Adrienne Anderson, Carrie Purcell**

Prop Stylist **Paige Hicks**

Designer **Susi Oberhelman**

Front cover: Macaroni and Cheese, page 52; Back cover: Super-Crispy Onion Rings, page 31; Tomato, Mushroom, and Pepperoni Pizzas, page 50; Cilantro Rice–Stuffed Poblanos, page 87; Classic Deviled Eggs, page 98; Mushroom and Golden Onion Bison Burgers, page 126; Pumpkin Seed–Bacon Praline, page 169; Big Blueberry Pie, page 180; and Devil's Food Cupcakes with White Icing Squiggles, page 215

CAPE COD CLAMBAKE, PAGE 142

ABOUT OUR RECIPES

While losing weight isn't only about what you eat, Weight Watchers realizes the critical role it plays in your success and overall good health. That's why our philosophy is to offer great-tasting, easy recipes that are nutritious as well as delicious. We make every attempt to use wholesome ingredients and to ensure that our recipes fall within the recommendations of the U.S. Dietary Guidelines for Americans for a diet that promotes health and reduces the risk for disease. If you have special dietary needs, consult with your health-care professional for advice on a diet that is best for you, then adapt these recipes to meet your specific nutritional needs.

To achieve these good-health goals and get the maximum satisfaction from the foods you eat, we suggest you keep the following information in mind while preparing our recipes:

THE PROGRAM AND GOOD NUTRITION

• Recipes in this book have been developed for Weight Watchers members who are following the *PointsPlus*® program. *PointsPlus* values are given for each recipe. They're assigned based on the amount of protein (grams), carbohydrates (grams), fat (grams), and fiber (grams) contained in a single serving of a recipe.

• Recipes include approximate nutritional information; they are analyzed for Calories (Cal), Total Fat, Saturated Fat (Sat Fat), Trans Fat, Cholesterol (Chol), Sodium (Sod), Carbohydrates (Carb), Sugar, Dietary Fiber (Fib), Protein (Prot), and Calcium (Calc). The nutritional values are calculated by registered dietitians, using nutrition analysis software.

• Substitutions made to the ingredients will alter the per-serving nutritional information and may affect the *PointsPlus* value.

• Our recipes meet Weight Watchers Good Health Guidelines for eating lean proteins and fiber-rich whole grains, and having at least five servings of vegetables and fruits and two servings of low-fat or fat-free dairy products a day, while limiting your intake of saturated fat, sugar, and sodium.

• Health agencies recommend limiting sodium intake. To stay in line with this recommendation we keep sodium levels in our recipes reasonably low; to boost flavor, we often include fresh herbs or a squeeze of citrus instead of salt. If you don't have to restrict your sodium, feel free to add a touch more salt as desired.

• In the recipes, a green triangle (▲) indicates Weight Watchers® Power Foods.

• FYI serving suggestions have a *PointsPlus* value of 0 unless otherwise stated.

• Recipes that work with the Simply Filling technique are listed on page 229. Find more details about this technique at your meeting.

• For information about the science behind lasting weight loss and more, please visit **WeightWatchers.com/science**.

CALCULATIONS NOT WHAT YOU EXPECTED?

• You might expect some of the *PointsPlus* values in this book to be lower when some of the foods they're made from, such as fruits and vegetables, have no *PointsPlus* values. Fruit and most veggies have no *PointsPlus* values when served as a snack or part of a meal, like a cup of berries with a sandwich. But if these foods are part of a recipe, their fiber and nutrient content are incorporated into the recipe calculations. These nutrients can affect the *PointsPlus* values.

• Alcohol is included in our *PointsPlus* calculations. Because alcohol information is generally not included on nutrition labels, it's not an option to include when using the hand calculator or the online calculator. But since we use alcohol information that we get from our nutritionists you might notice discrepancies between the *PointsPlus* values you see in our recipes, and the values you get using the calculator. The *PointsPlus* values listed for our recipes are the most accurate values.

SHOPPING FOR INGREDIENTS

As you learn to eat healthier and add more Weight Watchers Power Foods to your meals, remember these tips for choosing foods wisely:

Lean Meats and Poultry Purchase lean meats and poultry, and trim them of all visible fat before cooking. When poultry is cooked with the skin on, we recommend removing the skin before eating. Nutritional information for recipes that include meat, poultry, and fish is based on cooked, skinless boneless portions (unless otherwise stated), with the fat trimmed.

Seafood Whenever possible, our recipes call for seafood that is sustainable and deemed the most healthful for human consumption so that your choice of seafood is not only good for the oceans but also good for you. For more information about the best seafood choices and to download a pocket guide, go to **environmentaldefensefund. org** or **montereybayaquarium.org.** For information about mercury and seafood go to **Weight Watchers.com**.

Produce For best flavor, maximum nutrient content, and the lowest prices, buy fresh, local produce, such as vegetables, leafy greens, and fruits in season. Rinse them thoroughly before using and keep a supply of cut-up vegetables and fruits in your refrigerator for convenient, healthy snacks.

Whole Grains Explore your market for whole grain products such as whole wheat and whole grain breads and pastas, brown rice, bulgur, barley, cornmeal, whole wheat couscous, oats, and quinoa to enjoy with your meals.

PREPARATION AND MEASURING

Read the Recipe Take a couple of minutes to read through the ingredients and directions before you start to prepare a recipe. This will prevent you from discovering midway through that you don't have an important ingredient or that a recipe requires several hours of marinating. And it's also a good idea to assemble all ingredients and utensils within easy reach before you begin a recipe.

Weighing and Measuring The success of any recipe depends on accurate weighing and measuring. The effectiveness of the Weight Watchers program and the accuracy of the nutritional analysis depend on correct measuring as well. Use the following techniques:

• Weigh food such as meat, poultry, and fish on a food scale.

• To measure liquids, use a standard glass or plastic measuring cup placed on a level surface. For amounts less than $1/4$ cup, use standard measuring spoons.

• To measure dry ingredients, use metal or plastic measuring cups that come in $1/4$-, $1/3$-, $1/2$-, and 1-cup sizes. Fill the appropriate cup and level it with the flat edge of a knife or spatula. For amounts less than $1/4$ cup, use standard measuring spoons.

DEVIL'S FOOD CUPCAKES WITH
WHITE ICING SQUIGGLES, PAGE 215

CONTENTS

CRUNCHY AND CRISPY

SUPER-CRISPY ONION RINGS, PAGE 31

★ SALADS ★

Butternut Squash, Apple, and Raisin Slaw, 15

BLT Salad with Blue Cheese Dressing, 16

Cabbage Slaw with Lemony Buttermilk Dressing, 18

Three-Bean Salad, 19

★ MAIN DISHES ★

Oven-Fried Chicken, 21

Cornish Hens with Sage–Corn Bread Stuffing, 22

Turkey Tetrazzini, 23

Cornmeal-Coated Catfish, 24

Clams Casino, 27

Maryland-Style Crab Cakes, 29

★ SIDES ★

Fried Green Tomatoes, 30

Super-Crispy Onion Rings, 31

Steakhouse "Fries", 32

Red Flannel Hash, 33

★ BREADS ★

Johnnycakes with Warm Applesauce, 34

"Hushpuppy" Muffins, 35

Cheddar-Scallion Popovers, 36

Cast-Iron Skillet Corn Bread, 38

Toasted Sesame Cheese Straws, 39

BUTTERNUT SQUASH, APPLE, AND RAISIN SLAW

SERVES 6

To make dressing, whisk together coconut milk, ginger, lime zest and juice, brown sugar, harissa, and salt in serving bowl. Add squash, apple, and raisins; toss to coat evenly. Cover and refrigerate to allow flavors to blend, at least 1 hour or up to 3 hours. Serve sprinkled with coconut.

PER SERVING (about 1 cup): 99 Cal, 2 g Fat, 1 g Sat Fat, 0 g Trans Fat, 0 mg Chol, 104 mg Sod, 22 g Carb, 10 g sugar, 4 g Fib, 2 g Prot, 53 mg Calc.

¼ cup light (low-fat) coconut milk

1 tablespoon grated peeled fresh ginger

Grated zest and juice of 1 lime

2 teaspoons packed light brown sugar

1½ teaspoons harissa

¼ teaspoon salt

▲ 1 (1½-pound) butternut squash, peeled, seeded, and shredded (4 cups)

▲ 1 large Granny Smith apple, unpeeled, cored and cut into matchsticks

2 tablespoons golden raisins, chopped

2 tablespoons shredded unsweetened coconut, toasted

★ **FYI** ★ Raw butternut squash is crisp and has a subtle flavor that is the perfect complement to the apple, raisins, and coconut. Harissa is a super-hot sauce from Tunisia made from chiles, garlic, and spices. It is found in small brightly colored cans and tubes in specialty food stores and Middle Eastern markets.

BLT SALAD WITH BLUE CHEESE DRESSING

SERVES 4 | **20 MIN**

PER SERVING

⅓ cup low-fat buttermilk

▲ ⅓ cup fat-free sour cream

2 tablespoons red wine vinegar

1 tablespoon chopped fresh parsley

¼ teaspoon black pepper

½ cup crumbled reduced-fat blue cheese

▲ 1 small head iceberg lettuce, cut into 8 wedges

▲ 1 cup cherry tomatoes, halved

4 slices turkey bacon, crisp cooked and crumbled

1 To make dressing, whisk together buttermilk, sour cream, vinegar, parsley, and pepper in medium bowl. Stir in blue cheese.

2 Arrange 2 lettuce wedges on each of 4 plates. Scatter tomatoes around lettuce. Drizzle dressing evenly over lettuce and tomatoes; sprinkle evenly with bacon.

PER SERVING (2 lettuce wedges, ¼ cup tomatoes, 1 slice bacon, and about ¼ cup dressing): 138 Cal, 7 g Total Fat, 3 g Sat Fat, 0 g Trans Fat, 26 mg Chol, 513 mg Sod, 9 g Carb, 4 g Sugar, 1 g Fib, 11 g Prot, 172 mg Calc.

★ **FYI** ★ To add a bit of tempting bite to this salad, scatter 4 to 6 thinly sliced red radishes over the lettuce.

BLT SALAD WITH BLUE CHEESE DRESSING

CABBAGE SLAW WITH LEMONY BUTTERMILK DRESSING

SERVES 4

PER SERVING

⅓ cup reduced-fat mayonnaise

¼ cup low-fat buttermilk

1 tablespoon cider vinegar

1 tablespoon lemon juice

1 teaspoon sugar

½ teaspoon celery seeds

¼ teaspoon salt

▲ 1 (14-ounce) bag coleslaw mix

▲ 1 green bell pepper, finely chopped

▲ 3 scallions, thinly sliced

To make dressing, whisk together mayonnaise, buttermilk, vinegar, lemon juice, sugar, celery seeds, and salt in serving bowl. Add coleslaw mix, bell pepper, and scallions; toss to coat evenly. Cover and refrigerate at least 1 hour or up to 4 hours. Stir just before serving.

PER SERVING (1 cup): 79 Cal, 3 g Fat, 1 g Sat Fat, 0 g Trans Fat, 1 mg Chol, 357 mg Sod, 13 g Carb, 4 g sugar, 3 g Fib, 2 g Prot, 80 mg Calc.

★ **FYI** ★ If you happen to have some plain low-fat yogurt on hand, you can use it instead of the buttermilk.

THREE-BEAN SALAD

PER SERVING

1 Bring 1 inch of water to boil in medium saucepan. Add green beans and wax beans; cook, covered, until crisp-tender, about 6 minutes. Drain in colander and cool under cold running water.

2 To make dressing, whisk together vinegar, oil, sugar, salt, and black pepper in large bowl. Add green beans, wax beans, and remaining ingredients; toss until mixed well. Cover and refrigerate up to 6 hours.

PER SERVING (about ¾ cup): 125 Cal, 4 g Total Fat, 1 g Sat Fat, 0 g Trans Fat, 0 mg Chol, 150 mg Sod, 19 g Carb, 3 g Sugar, 7 g Fib, 5 g Prot, 25 mg Calc.

▲ ½ **pound green beans, trimmed and cut into 1-inch pieces**

▲ ½ **pound wax beans, trimmed and cut into 1-inch pieces**

¼ **cup cider vinegar**

2 **tablespoons olive oil**

1 **tablespoon sugar**

½ **teaspoon salt**

¼ **teaspoon black pepper**

▲ 1 (15½-ounce) can red kidney beans, rinsed and drained

▲ ½ **red bell pepper, chopped**

▲ ⅓ **cup chopped red onion**

2 **tablespoons chopped fresh parsley**

★ **FYI** ★ Add 1 cup halved or quartered red or yellow cherry tomatoes to the salad and serve with grilled or broiled arctic char fillets. Three ounces of cooked arctic char per serving will increase the **PointsPlus** value by **4.**

OVEN-FRIED CHICKEN

OVEN-FRIED CHICKEN

7
PointsPlus®
value

PER SERVING

1 Combine buttermilk, ½ teaspoon of pepper, and ¼ teaspoon of salt in large zip-close plastic bag; add chicken. Squeeze out air and seal bag; turn to coat chicken. Refrigerate, turning bag occasionally, at least 20 minutes or up to 3 hours.

2 Meanwhile, preheat oven to 350°F. Line baking sheet with foil and spray with nonstick spray.

3 Mix together bread crumbs, Parmesan, paprika, sage, rosemary, and remaining ½ teaspoon pepper and ¼ teaspoon salt in pie plate.

4 Remove chicken from buttermilk mixture. Discard buttermilk mixture. Coat chicken, one piece at a time, in bread crumb mixture. Place chicken on prepared baking sheet and bake 30 minutes. Remove baking sheet from oven and lightly spray chicken with nonstick spray. Return chicken to oven and bake until cooked through and crumbs are golden, about 15 minutes longer.

¾ cup low-fat buttermilk

1 teaspoon black pepper

½ teaspoon salt

▲ 4 (7-ounce) bone-in chicken breasts, skinned

1 cup whole wheat Panko (Japanese bread crumbs)

2 tablespoons grated Parmesan cheese

1 tablespoon paprika

2 teaspoons dried sage

1 teaspoon dried rosemary

PER SERVING (1 chicken breast): 306 Cal, 6 g Total Fat, 2 g Sat Fat, 0 g Trans Fat, 93 mg Chol, 488 mg Sod, 23 g Carb, 3 g Sugar, 4 g Fib, 39 g Prot, 112 mg Calc.

★ **FYI** ★ To turn this chicken into a Southern-style meal, serve it with steamed corn-on-the-cob and collard or mustard greens cooked in reduced-sodium chicken broth (1 medium ear of corn per serving will increase the **PointsPlus** value by **2**).

CORNISH HENS WITH SAGE-CORN BREAD STUFFING

SERVES 8

1 tablespoon olive oil

▲ 1 onion, chopped

▲ 2 celery stalks, chopped

▲ 1 carrot, grated

3 cups crumbled corn bread

▲ 1 large egg white, lightly beaten

1 teaspoon dried sage

¼ teaspoon salt

¼ teaspoon black pepper

▲ ½ cup reduced-sodium chicken broth

4 (1½-pound) Cornish hens, giblets removed

1 Preheat oven to 400°F.

2 To make stuffing, heat oil in large nonstick skillet over medium heat. Add onion, celery, and carrot; cook, stirring, until softened, about 5 minutes. Remove skillet from heat. Stir in corn bread, egg white, sage, salt, and pepper. Drizzle broth over stuffing and toss until moistened evenly.

3 Stuff each hen with one-fourth of stuffing (about ½ cup). Tie legs together with kitchen string. Place hens, breast side up, on rack in large roasting pan. Spray with olive oil nonstick spray. Roast until instant-read thermometer inserted into thigh (not touching bone) registers 165°F, about 45 minutes.

4 Let hens stand 10 minutes. With kitchen scissors, split each hen in half. Remove kitchen string and discard. Remove hen skin before eating.

PER SERVING (½ stuffed hen): 328 Cal, 10 g Total Fat, 2 g Sat Fat, 0 g Trans Fat, 163 mg Chol, 471 mg Sod, 22 g Carb, 2 g Sugar, 2 g Fib, 36 g Prot, 139 mg Calc.

★ **FYI** ★ *Poussins*, baby chickens, can be substituted for the Cornish hens, if you like.

TURKEY TETRAZZINI

PER SERVING

1 Preheat oven to 375°F. Spray 7 x 11-inch baking dish with nonstick spray.

2 Cook spaghetti according to package directions, omitting salt if desired. Drain and keep warm.

3 Stir together soup and milk in large bowl until smooth. Stir in turkey, roasted pepper, Parmesan, and black pepper; add spaghetti and stir until mixed well. Transfer to prepared baking dish.

4 Stir together bread crumbs and melted butter in small bowl until moistened; sprinkle over casserole. Bake until casserole is heated through and top is golden, about 25 minutes.

PER SERVING (about 1 cup): 322 Cal, 6 g Total Fat, 3 g Sat Fat, 0 g Trans Fat, 83 mg Chol, 634 mg Sod, 32 g Carb, 4 g Sugar, 4 g Fib, 35 g Prot, 133 mg Calc.

- 8 ounces whole wheat spaghetti
- 2 (10¾-ounce) cans reduced-fat condensed cream of mushroom soup
- 1 cup low-fat (1%) milk
- 3 cups cubed cooked skinless fat-free turkey breast
- ½ cup diced roasted red pepper (not packed in oil)
- ½ cup grated Parmesan cheese
- ¼ teaspoon black pepper
- ¼ cup Italian-seasoned dried whole wheat bread crumbs
- 1 tablespoon unsalted butter, melted

ALL AMERICAN

Turkey tetrazzini was created in the early 1900s in honor of soprano Luisa Tetrazzini, who debuted at the Metropolitan Opera House in New York in 1908. The Campbell's Soup Company is credited with popularizing this dish by reducing the number of ingredients and simplifying its method.

CORNMEAL-COATED CATFISH

SERVES 4

PER SERVING

¼ cup yellow cornmeal

2 tablespoons plain dried whole wheat bread crumbs

½ teaspoon dried oregano

½ teaspoon salt

¼ teaspoon black pepper

▲ 2 large egg whites

1 tablespoon water

6 drops hot pepper sauce or to taste

▲ 4 (¼-pound) catfish fillets

2 teaspoons canola oil

Lemon wedges

1 Mix together cornmeal, bread crumbs, oregano, salt, and black pepper on sheet of wax paper. Beat together egg whites, water, and pepper sauce in pie plate.

2 Dip catfish fillets, one at a time, in egg white mixture. Coat each fillet with cornmeal mixture, shaking off excess.

3 Heat oil in large nonstick skillet over medium-high heat. Cook fish, in batches if needed, until just opaque throughout, about 3 minutes per side. Serve with lemon wedges.

PER SERVING (1 catfish fillet): 212 Cal, 9 g Total Fat, 2 g Sat Fat, 0 g Trans Fat, 51 mg Chol, 404 mg Sod, 10 g Carb, 1 g Sugar, 1 g Fib, 20 g Prot, 13 mg Calc.

★ **FYI** ★ Serve the fish with steamed green beans and red bell pepper and steamed halved baby potatoes lightly sprayed with nonstick spray and sprinkled with chopped fresh parsley (3 ounces of steamed baby potatoes per serving will increase the *PointsPlus* value by **2**).

CORNMEAL-COATED CATFISH

ADD CRUNCH WITH
HOMEMADE BREAD CRUMBS

Homemade bread crumbs, whether fresh or dried, plain or seasoned, fine or coarse, add texture, flavor, and visual appeal to all kinds of foods without a lot of time or fuss. Even though it is easy to pick up a package of ready-made crumbs from your supermarket, they taste fresher and more flavorful when prepared at home. Fresh bread crumbs are great for stuffing into vegetables and for ground meat or poultry mixtures, while dried bread crumbs are ideal for sprinkling over or layering in casseroles. Using whole wheat bread for bread crumbs is an easy, tasty way to incorporate whole grains into your diet.

• **Fresh bread crumbs** are best made with day-old bread. Use whole wheat, sourdough, French, or Italian bread. Cut off the crust and discard, then cut or tear the bread into 1-inch chunks. Put the chunks into a food processor and pulse until coarse crumbs form. It takes about 1 slice of bread to make ½ cup of crumbs. To make a small amount of crumbs, cut off the crust from a chunk of day-old bread, then grate the bread on the large holes of a box grater.
STORAGE: Transfer the crumbs to a covered container and refrigerate up to 5 days, or for longer storage, transfer the crumbs to a zip-close plastic freezer bag and freeze up to 2 months.

• **Plain dried bread crumbs** can be fine or coarse. Preheat the oven to 375°F. Slice whole wheat, sourdough, French, or Italian bread and arrange in one layer on a baking sheet. Bake until deep golden on both sides, about 10 minutes. Turn off the oven and prop the oven door open with the handle of a wooden spoon. Let the bread remain in the oven until very dry and crisp, about 15 minutes. When the slices are completely cool, crush them with your hands and put into a food processor, in batches if needed. Process until they form coarse or fine crumbs.
STORAGE: Transfer the crumbs to a covered container and refrigerate up to 1 week. For longer storage, put the crumbs into a zip-close plastic freezer bag and freeze up to 3 months.

• **Seasoned dried bread crumbs** are easy to make. First make a batch of plain dried bread crumbs as directed above. Transfer the crumbs to a bowl. Season them by adding a small amount of dried oregano, basil, thyme or a combination, along with garlic powder, paprika, black pepper and, if desired, some finely grated Parmesan cheese. Taste the crumb mixture and re-season if needed.
STORAGE: Transfer the crumbs to a covered container and refrigerate up to 1 week. For longer storage, put the crumbs into a zip-close plastic freezer bag and freeze up to 3 months.

• **Seasoned panko (Japanese) bread crumbs** are a snap to make at home. The super-crisp flakes come in plain and whole wheat versions. To season, measure the amount needed and season with any favorite dried herbs, such as oregano or thyme, then add onion or garlic powder and black pepper. For a lively fresh flavor, toss in a bit of finely grated lemon peel. Toss well and taste. Re-season if needed.
STORAGE: Transfer the panko to a covered container and refrigerate up to 1 week. For longer storage, put the panko into a zip-close plastic freezer bag and freeze up to 3 months.

CLAMS CASINO

1 Preheat oven to 450°F. Line baking sheet with foil.

2 Cook bacon in medium nonstick skillet until crisp. With slotted spoon, transfer bacon to paper towel–lined plate to drain.

3 Spray skillet with nonstick spray. Add bell pepper, onion, parsley, and garlic; cook, stirring, until onion is softened, about 5 minutes. Stir in Parmesan, oregano, black pepper, and pepper flakes. Crumble bacon and stir into vegetable mixture.

4 Put clams in bottom shells and place on prepared baking sheet; top clams evenly with bacon mixture. Bake until clams are just cooked through and topping is golden, about 8 minutes. Serve with lemon wedges.

PER SERVING (8 clams): 215 Cal, 8 g Total Fat, 3 g Sat Fat, 0 g Trans Fat, 71 mg Chol, 533 mg Sod, 8 g Carb, 2 g Sugar, 1 g Fib, 27 g Prot, 158 mg Calc.

4 slices turkey bacon

▲ 1 small red bell pepper, finely chopped

▲ 1 small onion, finely chopped

2 tablespoons chopped fresh parsley

2 large garlic cloves, minced

⅓ cup grated Parmesan cheese

½ teaspoon dried oregano

¼ teaspoon black pepper

Pinch red pepper flakes

▲ 32 littleneck clams, scrubbed, shucked, and bottom shells reserved

Lemon wedges

ALL AMERICAN

As the story goes, clams casino was created in 1917 by Julius Keller, maître d'hotel of the Casino restaurant at Narragansett Pier in New York City, for a luncheon that socialite Mrs. Paran Stevens was hosting. It quickly became popular and has remained so to this day. Here it has been turned into a delicious main dish.

MARYLAND-STYLE CRAB CAKES

SERVES 4

1 Gently stir together crabmeat, mayonnaise, chives, mustard, lemon juice, black pepper, and pepper sauce in medium bowl. Shape mixture into 8 patties. Spread bread crumbs on sheet of wax paper. Coat each patty in crumbs, pressing gently so they adhere.
2 Heat oil in large nonstick skillet over medium heat. Add patties, in batches if needed and cook until browned and heated through, about 5 minutes per side. Serve with lemon wedges.

PER SERVING (2 crab cakes): 198 Cal, 8 g Total Fat, 2 g Sat Fat, 0 g Trans Fat, 87 mg Chol, 711 mg Sod, 8 g Carb, 2 g Sugar, 0 g Fib, 26 g Prot, 107 mg Calc.

- 1 pound lump crabmeat, picked over
- 3 tablespoons reduced-fat mayonnaise
- 2 tablespoons snipped fresh chives
- 1 tablespoon Dijon mustard
- 2 teaspoons lemon juice
- ¼ teaspoon black pepper
- Few drops hot pepper sauce
- ⅓ cup plain dried whole wheat bread crumbs
- 1 tablespoon canola oil
- Lemon wedges

ALL AMERICAN

It is believed that Lord Baltimore, founding father of the state of Maryland, dined on crab cakes in the 1630s. It wasn't until some 300 years later, however, that the term *crab cake* first appeared in print.

FRIED GREEN TOMATOES

½ cup yellow cornmeal

½ cup grated Parmesan cheese

½ teaspoon dried thyme

½ teaspoon black pepper

¼ teaspoon salt

Pinch cayenne

▲ 3 large green tomatoes, each cut into 4 (½-inch) slices

1 Mix together cornmeal, Parmesan, thyme, black pepper, salt, and cayenne on sheet of wax paper. Coat tomato slices, one at a time, in cornmeal mixture, pressing so it adheres.

2 Spray large heavy skillet with nonstick spray and set over medium-high heat. Add tomatoes, in batches, and cook until golden brown, about 4 minutes per side, spraying skillet with nonstick spray between batches.

PER SERVING (3 tomato slices): 150 Cal, 3 g Total Fat, 2 g Sat Fat, 0 g Trans Fat, 9 mg Chol, 318 mg Sod, 24 g Carb, 6 g Sugar, 2 g Fib, 7 g Prot, 132 mg Calc.

★ **FYI** ★ Green tomatoes are readily available in farmers' markets in late summer. Unripe firm red tomatoes can also be used—or use a combination of red and green.

SUPER-CRISPY ONION RINGS

1 Preheat oven to 450°F. Spray two large baking sheets with nonstick spray.

2 Put flour in large zip-close plastic bag. Whisk together buttermilk and pepper in shallow bowl. Spread bread crumbs on sheet of wax paper.

3 Add onion rings, a few at a time, to flour; seal bag and shake until onion rings are coated evenly. Dip rings, one at a time, in buttermilk mixture, then coat with bread crumbs; transfer rings to prepared baking sheets. Bake until golden and crispy, about 20 minutes.

⅓ cup all-purpose flour

1 cup low-fat buttermilk

½ teaspoon black pepper

½ cup Italian-seasoned dried bread crumbs

▲ 2 large onions, cut crosswise into ½-inch rounds and separated into 32 rings

PER SERVING (8 onion rings): 162 g, 149 Cal, 2 g Total Fat, 1 g Sat Fat, 0 g Trans Fat, 2 mg Chol, 449 mg Sod, 28 g Carb, 7 g Sugar, 2 g Fib, 6 g Prot, 111 mg Calc.

★ **FYI** ★ To add a bit of smokiness to these crispy onion rings, add about 1 teaspoon of smoked paprika, also known as *pimentón*, to the bread crumbs.

STEAKHOUSE "FRIES"

PER SERVING

2 teaspoons chili powder

2 teaspoons smoked paprika

2 teaspoons onion powder

1 teaspoon dried oregano, crumbled

½ teaspoon salt

½ teaspoon black pepper

▲ 2 (10-ounce) baking potatoes, scrubbed and each cut into 8 wedges

1 Preheat oven to 425°F. Spray baking sheet with nonstick spray.

2 Stir together chili powder, paprika, onion powder, oregano, salt, and pepper in cup. Put potatoes in large bowl and spray with nonstick spray, tossing until coated evenly. Sprinkle spice mixture over potatoes, tossing as you go.

3 Arrange potatoes, skin side down, on prepared baking sheet. Bake until tender and nicely browned, about 25 minutes.

PER SERVING (4 potato wedges): 110 Cal, 1 g Total Fat, 0 g Sat Fat, 0 g Trans Fat, 0 mg Chol, 307 mg Sod, 27 g Carb, 3 g Sugar, 4 g Fib, 4 g Prot, 33 mg Calc.

★ **FYI** ★ Sweet potatoes can be substituted for the baking potatoes. Or use one baking potato and one sweet potato.

RED FLANNEL HASH

PER SERVING

1 Spray 10-inch nonstick or cast-iron skillet with nonstick spray and set over medium heat. Add cabbage and cook, stirring, until wilted, about 5 minutes. Transfer to large bowl. Stir in potatoes, beets, onion, salt, and pepper.

2 Heat 2 teaspoons of oil in skillet over medium heat. Add potato mixture, pressing it down with pancake spatula. Drizzle with ⅓ cup of broth. Cook, shaking pan occasionally to prevent sticking, until crisp and browned on bottom, about 12 minutes.

3 Remove skillet from heat. Invert large plate on top of skillet. Wearing oven mitts, turn skillet over. Add remaining 1 teaspoon oil to skillet; slide hash pancake back into skillet. Drizzle with remaining ⅓ cup broth. Cook, shaking pan occasionally, until crisp and browned on bottom, about 10 minutes longer. Cut into 4 wedges.

- ▲ 2 cups chopped green or red cabbage
- ▲ 1½ pounds all-purpose potatoes, peeled, chopped, and cooked
- ▲ 1½ cups packaged or drained canned cooked beets, chopped
- ▲ 1 small onion, chopped
- ½ teaspoon salt
- ¼ teaspoon black pepper
- 3 teaspoons canola oil
- ▲ ⅔ cup reduced-sodium chicken broth

PER SERVING (1 wedge): 216 Cal, 4 g Total Fat, 0 g Sat Fat, 0 g Trans Fat, 0 mg Chol, 380 mg Sod, 41 g Carb, 9 g Sugar, 6 g Fib, 6 g Prot, 57 mg Calc.

★ **FYI** ★ Top each serving of hash with a poached egg for a satisfying breakfast or brunch. One poached large egg per serving will increase the *PointsPlus* value by *2*.

JOHNNYCAKES WITH WARM APPLESAUCE

6 PointsPlus® value

PER SERVING

APPLESAUCE

▲ 3 McIntosh apples, peeled, cored, and cut into chunks

¼ cup water

1 tablespoon sugar

Juice of ½ lemon

JOHNNYCAKES

¾ cup flint or white cornmeal

▲ ¾ cup fat-free milk

▲ 1 large egg, lightly beaten

¾ teaspoon salt

1 To make applesauce, combine apples, water, sugar, and lemon juice in medium saucepan over medium heat. Cook, stirring to prevent apples from sticking, until apples are very soft, about 15 minutes. Remove saucepan from heat.

2 To make johnnycakes, whisk together cornmeal, milk, egg, and salt in medium bowl. Let batter stand about 15 minutes.

3 Generously spray nonstick griddle or large nonstick skillet with nonstick spray and set over medium heat. Drop ⅛ cupfuls of batter onto griddle, making total of 8 johnnycakes. Cook until bubbles appear and edges of pancakes look dry, about 2 minutes. Turn pancakes over and cook until golden on second side, about 2 minutes longer. Serve with applesauce.

PER SERVING (2 johnnycakes and about ⅓ cup applesauce): 219 Cal, 1 g Total Fat, 0 g Sat Fat, 0 g Trans Fat, 55 mg Chol, 472 mg Sod, 47 g Carb, 16 g Sugar, 2 g Fib, 5 g Prot, 70 mg Calc.

ALL AMERICAN

Johnnycakes, a Rhode Island institution, are thin, flat pancakes traditionally made from ground Indian corn, also known as flint corn. Food purists insist that only flint cornmeal can be used to make authentic Johnnycakes, but white cornmeal makes a fine substitution.

"HUSHPUPPY" MUFFINS

SERVES 6

1 Spray two 12-cup mini muffin pans with nonstick spray. Place in oven and preheat oven to 450°F.

2 Whisk together cornmeal, flour, sugar, baking powder, salt, baking soda, and pepper in medium bowl. Whisk together buttermilk, egg, and onion in small bowl. Add buttermilk mixture to cornmeal mixture, stirring just until cornmeal mixture is moistened.

3 Wearing oven mitts, remove muffin pans from oven. Spoon batter evenly into prepared cups, filling each about three-fourths full.

4 Bake until toothpick inserted into center of hushpuppy comes out clean, about 10 minutes. Run thin knife around sides of muffin cups to release hushpuppies. Serve hot or warm.

¾ cup cornmeal

¼ cup all-purpose flour

1 teaspoon sugar

½ teaspoon baking powder

½ teaspoon salt

¼ teaspoon baking soda

⅛ teaspoon black pepper

¾ cup low-fat buttermilk

▲ 1 large egg

▲ 2 tablespoons finely grated onion

PER SERVING (4 hushpuppies): 103 Cal, 2 g Total Fat, 0 g Sat Fat, 0 g Trans Fat, 37 mg Chol, 340 mg Sod, 18 g Carb, 2 g Sugar, 3 g Fib, 4 g Prot, 54 mg Calc.

ALL AMERICAN

There are several stories regarding how these delectable balls of dough got their name. As one story goes, when hounds were taken along on fishing expeditions, they would yelp when they smelled fish being fried. To quiet them, the fishermen would toss the dogs bits of the fried dough. Though traditionally fried, our baked hushpuppies are just as delicious.

CHEDDAR-SCALLION POPOVERS

3
PointsPlus®
value

PER SERVING

1⅔ cups low-fat (1%) milk

1½ cups all-purpose flour

▲ 3 large eggs

1 teaspoon salt

¼ teaspoon cayenne

1½ cups shredded reduced-fat Cheddar cheese

▲ ½ cup finely chopped scallions (about 4 scallions)

1 Preheat oven to 450°F. Lightly spray 12-cup popover or jumbo muffin pan with nonstick spray.

2 Combine milk, flour, eggs, salt, and cayenne in blender; blend until smooth. Pour into large bowl.

3 Stir 1 cup of Cheddar and the scallions into batter. Pour ⅓ cupfuls of batter into prepared popover cups. Sprinkle evenly with remaining ½ cup Cheddar.

4 Bake popovers 15 minutes. Reduce oven to 375°F and bake until golden brown, 8–10 minutes longer. Serve hot.

PER SERVING (1 popover): 115 Cal, 3 g Total Fat, 1 g Sat Fat, 0 g Trans Fat, 58 mg Chol, 312 mg Sod, 14 g Carb, 2 g Sugar, 1 g Fib, 8 g Prot, 110 mg Calc.

ALL AMERICAN

Most food historians agree that popovers are a close cousin to English Yorkshire pudding. According to Evan Jones, author of *American Food* (1974), the settlers who founded Portland, Oregon, Americanized Yorkshire pudding by cooking it in cups instead of in a roasting pan and called it Portland popover pudding. The batter can be prepared several hours ahead and refrigerated.

CHEDDAR-SCALLION POPOVERS

CAST-IRON SKILLET CORN BREAD

SERVES 12

1½ cups stone-ground cornmeal

¾ cup all-purpose flour

2 tablespoons sugar

1½ teaspoons baking powder

½ teaspoon baking soda

½ teaspoon salt

1½ cups low-fat buttermilk

▲ 2 large egg whites

▲ 1 large egg

3 tablespoons canola oil

1 Place 9-inch cast-iron skillet in oven and preheat oven to 425°F.

2 Whisk together cornmeal, flour, sugar, baking powder, baking soda, and salt in medium bowl. Whisk together buttermilk, egg whites, egg, and 2 tablespoons of oil in small bowl. Add buttermilk mixture to cornmeal mixture, stirring just until cornmeal mixture is moistened.

3 Wearing oven mitts, remove skillet from oven. Add remaining 1 tablespoon oil to skillet and brush to coat bottom of skillet. Pour in batter and gently shake pan to spread evenly.

4 Bake corn bread until crisp along edge and toothpick inserted into center comes out clean, 20–25 minutes. Let cool in pan on wire rack 10 minutes. Cut into 12 wedges.

PER SERVING (1 wedge): 141 Cal, 5 g Total Fat, 1 g Sat Fat, 0 g Trans Fat, 19 mg Chol, 270 mg Sod, 21 g Carb, 3 g Sugar, 3 g Fib, 4 g Prot, 56 mg Calc.

ALL AMERICAN

Native Americans were making corn bread, which they called pone, long before the first settlers came to America. These early breads were a simple mixture of cornmeal, salt, and water. Nowadays corn bread is prepared either Northern style or Southern style: Northern-style corn bread contains a high proportion of flour to cornmeal and some sugar, while Southern-style corn bread often doesn't include flour or sugar.

TOASTED SESAME CHEESE STRAWS

1 Preheat oven to 400°F. Spray nonstick baking sheet with nonstick spray.

2 Toss together Parmesan, sesame seeds, and paprika in small bowl. Whisk together egg white, oil, and water in another small bowl.

3 Place one sheet of phyllo on work surface with short side facing you. (Cover remaining phyllo with damp paper towels to prevent it from drying out.) Brush egg-white mixture over lower half of phyllo and sprinkle with 2 teaspoons of Parmesan mixture. Fold unfilled half of phyllo over filled half, forming 8½ x 12-inch rectangle. Brush right half of phyllo with egg-white mixture and sprinkle with 2 teaspoons of cheese mixture. Fold unfilled half of phyllo over filled half, forming 6 x 8½-inch rectangle. Brush bottom half of phyllo with egg-white mixture and sprinkle with 2 teaspoons of cheese mixture. Fold unfilled half of phyllo over filled half, forming 4¼ x 6-inch rectangle. To finish, brush phyllo with egg-white mixture and sprinkle with 2 teaspoons of cheese mixture. With pizza cutter or sharp knife, cut phyllo crosswise (short way) into 8 strips.

4 Transfer strips to prepared baking sheet about ½ inch apart. Repeat with remaining phyllo, egg-white mixture, and cheese mixture, making total of 24 cheese straws.

5 Bake until cheese straws are crisp and golden, 8–10 minutes. Transfer to wire racks and let cool completely.

½ cup grated Parmesan or Asiago cheese

2½ teaspoons toasted sesame seeds

¼ teaspoon hot paprika or cayenne

▲ 1 large egg white

1 tablespoon (Asian) sesame oil

½ teaspoon water

3 (12 x 17-inch) sheets frozen phyllo dough, thawed

PER SERVING (3 cheese straws): 66 Cal, 4 g Total Fat, 1 g Sat Fat, 0 g Trans Fat, 4 mg Chol, 120 mg Sod, 4 g Carb, 0 g Sugar, 0 g Fib, 3 g Prot, 60 mg Calc.

★ **FYI** ★ Toasted sesame seeds are available in the spice aisle of supermarkets.

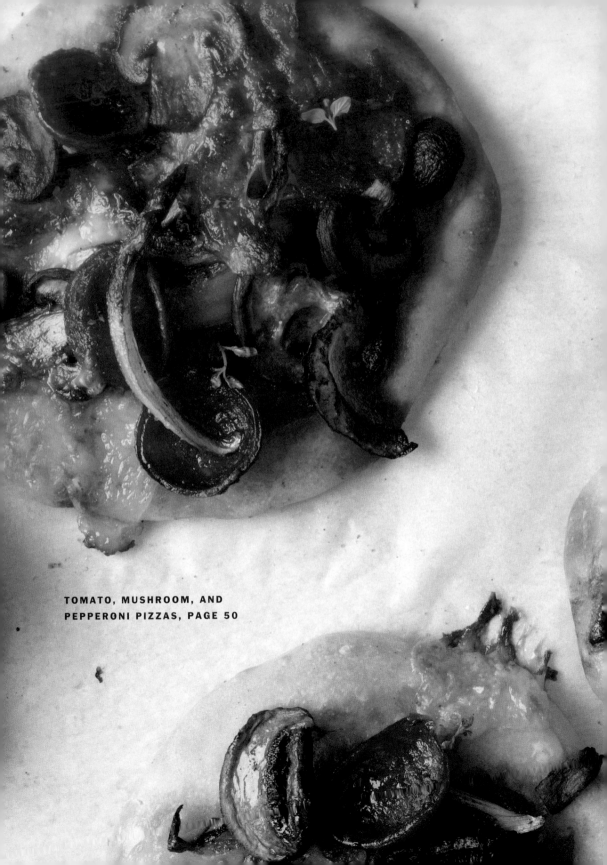

TOMATO, MUSHROOM, AND
PEPPERONI PIZZAS, PAGE 50

CHEESY

★ LUNCHES ★

Philly Cheesesteak Sandwiches, 43

Kentucky Hot Browns, 44

Open-Face Tuna Melts, 46

Vegetable Quesadillas, 47

Double Cheese Burritos, 49

Tomato, Mushroom, and Pepperoni Pizzas, 50

Macaroni and Cheese, 52

Penne with Tomatoes, Red Onion, and Blue Cheese, 54

Creamy Cheddar Cheese Soup, 55

Wild Mushroom and Feta Cheese Frittata, 56

★ SIDES ★

Twice-Baked Potatoes with Crispy Prosciutto and
Goat Cheese, 57

Classic Scalloped Potatoes, 59

Mixed Greens with Pecans, Goat Cheese, and
Dried Cranberries, 60

Warm Spinach, Mushroom, and Bacon Salad, 62

Cheddar-Rosemary Biscuits, 63

PHILLY CHEESESTEAK SANDWICHES

8
PointsPlus®
value

PER SERVING

1 Preheat boiler. Spray broiler rack with nonstick spray.

2 Spray large nonstick skillet with nonstick spray and set over medium-high heat. Add beef and cook, turning, until browned, about 4 minutes. Transfer to plate.

3 Spray skillet with nonstick spray. Add bell pepper, onion, and garlic; cook, stirring, until onion is softened, about 5 minutes. Return beef to skillet along with Worcestershire sauce and pepper sauce; cook until heated through, about 2 minutes longer.

4 Place rolls, cut sides up, on prepared broiler rack. Broil 5 inches from heat until toasted.

5 Spoon ½ cup of beef mixture over bottom of each roll. Top each with 1 slice of American cheese. Broil until cheese is melted, 1–2 minutes. Cover with tops of rolls.

- ½ pound top round steak, trimmed and thinly sliced
- 1 red bell pepper, cut into thin strips
- 1 onion, thinly sliced

  2 large garlic cloves, minced

  1 tablespoon Worcestershire sauce

  ½ teaspoon hot pepper sauce

  4 (2-ounce) whole wheat rolls, split and doughy centers removed

  4 (½-ounce) slices reduced-fat American cheese, cut into strips

PER SERVING (1 sandwich): 294 Cal, 9 g Total Fat, 4 g Sat Fat, 0 g Trans Fat, 32 mg Chol, 565 mg Sod, 36 g Carb, 9 g Sugar, 6 g Fib, 21 g Prot, 153 mg Calc.

ALL AMERICAN

In the 1930s, Philadelphia restaurant owner Pat Olivieri enticed customers by serving up fried steak and onions on a crusty hero roll. In time, he added bell peppers and American cheese to the sandwich, making it even more popular.

KENTUCKY HOT BROWNS

▲ 1 cup fat-free milk

2 tablespoons all-purpose flour

½ cup shredded reduced-fat Cheddar cheese

4 tablespoons grated Parmesan cheese

¼ teaspoon hot pepper sauce, such as Frank's

4 slices whole wheat bread, toasted and cut in half on diagonal

▲ ½ pound thinly sliced cooked skinless fat-free turkey breast

▲ 8 tomato slices

4 slices turkey bacon, crisp cooked

Paprika

1 tablespoon chopped fresh parsley

1 Whisk together milk and flour in small saucepan until smooth. Cook over medium heat, stirring frequently, until sauce bubbles and thickens. Reduce heat and simmer 3 minutes. Remove saucepan from heat and add Cheddar, 2 tablespoons of Parmesan, and the pepper sauce; stir until Cheddar is melted and cheese sauce is smooth.

2 Preheat broiler.

3 Overlap 2 half-slices of toast in each of 4 individual casserole dishes or other ovenproof dishes. Layer turkey, tomato, and bacon on top of bread. Top evenly with cheese sauce and sprinkle with remaining 2 tablespoons Parmesan. Lightly dust with paprika.

4 Place dishes on baking sheet and broil 5 inches from heat until sauce is browned in spots. Sprinkle with parsley.

PER SERVING (1 sandwich): 290 Cal, 8 g Total Fat, 3 g Sat Fat, 0 g Trans Fat, 69 mg Chol, 681 mg Sod, 21 g Carb, 6 g Sugar, 3 g Fib, 33 g Prot, 236 mg Calc.

ALL AMERICAN

In the late 1920s, this hot open-face sandwich was created by the chef at the Brown Hotel in Louisville, Kentucky. It was a quick and satisfying way to appease hungry travelers upon their arrival to the hotel.

KENTUCKY HOT BROWNS

OPEN-FACE TUNA MELTS

SERVES 4 20 MIN

▲ 1 (5-ounce) can light tuna packed in water, drained

¼ cup reduced-fat mayonnaise

▲ 1 celery stalk, finely chopped

▲ ¼ cup finely chopped red bell pepper

▲ 2 tablespoons finely chopped onion

1 tablespoon lemon juice

¼ teaspoon black pepper

2 whole wheat English muffins, split and toasted

▲ 4 thick tomato slices

4 (¾-ounce) slices reduced-fat Swiss cheese

1 Preheat broiler.

2 Flake tuna into medium bowl. Add mayonnaise, celery, bell pepper, onion, lemon juice, and black pepper; stir until mixed well.

3 Spread tuna mixture evenly on English muffins; top each with 1 slice of tomato and 1 slice of Swiss cheese.

4 Place sandwiches on rack of broiler pan. Broil 5 inches from heat until cheese is melted, about 2 minutes.

PER SERVING (1 sandwich): 211 Cal, 7 g Total Fat, 3 g Sat Fat, 0 g Trans Fat, 33 mg Chol, 520 mg Sod, 19 g Carb, 5 g Sugar, 3 g Fib, 20 g Prot, 300 mg Calc.

★ **FYI** ★ To add some zing to this classic sandwich, serve it with sugar-free pickle spears.

VEGETABLE QUESADILLAS

5
PointsPlus®
value

PER SERVING

1 Toss together tomatoes, mushrooms, bell pepper, scallions, and jalapeño in medium bowl.

2 Lay tortillas on work surface. Spoon one-fourth of vegetable mixture over one half of each tortilla. Sprinkle each with 1 tablespoon of Monterey Jack. Fold unfilled half of each tortilla over filling and press down lightly.

3 Spray large nonstick skillet with nonstick spray and set over medium-high heat. Place 2 quesadillas in skillet and cook until browned in spots, about 2 minutes. Spray tops of tortillas with nonstick spray; turn quesadillas over and cook until cheese is melted and tortillas are browned in spots on second side.

4 Transfer quesadillas to platter and keep warm. Spray skillet with nonstick spray and cook remaining quesadillas.

▲ 4 plum tomatoes, chopped

▲ 8 white mushrooms, thinly sliced

▲ 1 small red bell pepper, chopped

▲ 3 scallions, thinly sliced

▲ 1 jalapeño pepper, seeded and minced

4 (8-inch) reduced-fat whole wheat tortillas

4 tablespoons shredded reduced-fat Monterey Jack cheese

PER SERVING (1 quesadilla): 200 Cal, 6 g Total Fat, 2 g Sat Fat, 0 g Trans Fat, 8 mg Chol, 525 mg Sod, 29 g Carb, 5 g Sugar, 7 g Fib, 8 g Prot, 218 mg Calc.

★ **FYI** ★ To make these quesadillas even heartier, arrange cooked peeled and deveined medium shrimp over the vegetable mixture. Two ounces of cooked medium or large shrimp per serving will increase the *PointsPlus* value by *1*.

DOUBLE CHEESE BURRITOS

DOUBLE CHEESE BURRITOS

5 PointsPlus® value

PER SERVING

20 MIN   **SERVES 4**

1 Spray large nonstick skillet with nonstick spray and set over medium heat. Add egg substitute and sprinkle with pepper. Cook until eggs begin to set, about 1½ minutes, pushing egg mixture toward center of skillet to form large, soft curds. Continue cooking until eggs are just set, about 3 minutes longer.

2 Divide egg mixture, salsa, Monterey Jack, Cheddar, scallions, and cilantro evenly among tortillas. Top each with an avocado wedge. Fold two opposite sides of each tortilla over to enclose filling.

PER SERVING (1 burrito): 201 Cal, 7 g Total Fat, 3 g Sat Fat, 0 g Trans Fat, 10 mg Chol, 480 mg Sod, 23 g Carb, 2 g Sugar, 4 g Fib, 13 g Prot, 277 mg Calc.

▲ 1½ cups fat-free egg substitute

⅛ teaspoon black pepper

4 (6-inch) reduced-fat whole wheat tortillas, warmed

▲ 1 cup fat-free salsa

8 tablespoons shredded reduced-fat Monterey Jack cheese

8 tablespoons shredded reduced-fat sharp Cheddar cheese

▲ 2 scallions, sliced

4 tablespoons fresh cilantro leaves

½ Hass avocado, pitted, peeled, and cut into 4 wedges

★ **FYI** ★ To add some crunch to these burritos, dice half of a small red bell pepper and divide evenly among the burritos.

TOMATO, MUSHROOM, AND PEPPERONI PIZZAS

SERVES 6 ....

PER SERVING

2 teaspoons olive oil

▲ 1 pound cremini mushrooms, thinly sliced

▲ 1 large onion, thinly sliced

2 garlic cloves, minced

½ teaspoon dried thyme

1 pound refrigerated or thawed frozen whole wheat pizza dough

▲ ¾ cup chopped Italian tomatoes (such as Pomi)

24 slices turkey pepperoni

16 tablespoons shredded part-skim mozzarella cheese

1 Place one rack on bottom rung of oven and one rack in middle of oven. Preheat oven to 450°F. Sprinkle two baking sheets with cornmeal.

2 Heat oil in large nonstick skillet over medium-high heat. Add mushrooms, onion, garlic, and thyme; cook, stirring occasionally, until mushroom liquid is evaporated and mushrooms are browned, about 8 minutes. Remove skillet from heat; let cool slightly.

3 Divide dough into 6 equal pieces. Lightly sprinkle work surface with flour. With lightly floured rolling pin, roll out each piece of dough to 4-inch round. Transfer rounds of dough to prepared baking sheets. Spread 2 tablespoons of tomatoes over each round. Top each with ¼ cup of mushroom mixture, 4 pepperoni slices, and generous 2 tablespoons of mozzarella.

4 Bake pizzas until mozzarella is melted and crust is browned 15–20 minutes, rotating baking sheets after 8 minutes of baking time.

PER SERVING (1 pizza): 293 Cal, 8 g Fat, 3 g Sat Fat, 0 g Trans Fat, 17 mg Chol, 487 mg Sod, 40 g Carb, 5 g Fib, 14 g Prot, 191 mg Calc.

CHEESE IT TO THE MAX!

American cheese-making dates back to the first colonists. In 1620, the Mayflower's cargo included goats whose milk was used for goat cheese that was likely enjoyed during the first Thanksgiving. By 1624, cows were brought to America and cheese-making began in earnest.

Storage: Fresh cheese, such as ricotta, should be refrigerated in its original container in the refrigerator up to 3 weeks. **Soft** cheese, such as goat cheese and mozzarella, can be stored tightly wrapped in the refrigerator up to 2 weeks. **Semi-firm and firm** cheeses, such as blue cheese, Cheddar and Parmesan, should be tightly wrapped in wax paper, placed in a zip-close plastic bag, and refrigerated up to 2 months.

Mold: Trim away mold from soft, semi-firm, or hard cheeses and discard. Do not eat fresh cheese that develops mold.

NAME	DESCRIPTION	BEST USES
Blue Cheese	Maytag Blue, the best-known American blue cheese, is produced in Iowa. During the cheese-making process the curds (solids) are separated from the whey (liquid). Salt and bacterium from the penicillum family are then combined with the curds which are then packed into molds, where this cheese's characteristic flavor and texture have time to develop.	salad dressing, salads, stuffed into burgers, spread on crackers
Cheddar	This favorite cheese has its origins in Cheddar, England. It is a firm cow's milk cheese that ranges in flavor (determined by how long it ages) from mild to extra-sharp and in color from natural white to bright orange. The flavor of cheddar depends upon how long it is aged. With time it loses moisture and develops its characteristic slightly crumbly texture.	burger toppings, sandwiches, paninis, main-dish salads, vegetable casseroles, mac and cheese, quesadillas
Mozzarella	Besides the regular mozzarella sold in tightly wrapped packages, there are also fresh mozzarella balls packed in small containers containing brine. For a true eating experience, however, look for handmade mozzarella sold in Italian food stores. This hand-pulled cheese, made daily, is best eaten within a day or two.	pizza, paninis, pasta, tomato salad, casseroles
Parmesan	Though no Parmesan can compare with authentic imported Parmesan-Reggiano, good Parmesan is produced in Wisconsin and New York. It is sold in rectangular blocks in supermarkets. You can easily grate Parmesan in a food processor or with a box or Microplane grater.	pizza, pasta, vegetables, mashed potatoes, topping for soup
Ricotta	Ricotta, which means "twice cooked," is made from leftover whey. Most ricotta is made from cow's milk, though there are a few farms that make it the authentic Italian way—from sheep's milk.	lasagna, omelettes, frittatas, cheesecake

MACARONI AND CHEESE

▲ 8 ounces whole wheat elbow macaroni

1 tablespoon unsalted butter

▲ 1 small onion, chopped

1 tablespoon all-purpose flour

▲ 1½ cups fat-free milk

1 cup shredded reduced-fat Cheddar cheese

½ teaspoon salt

¼ teaspoon mustard powder

¼ teaspoon black pepper

¼ cup plain dried whole wheat bread crumbs

1 Preheat oven to 350°F. Spray 9-inch square baking dish with nonstick spray.

2 Cook macaroni according to package directions, omitting salt if desired. Drain.

3 Meanwhile, melt butter in large saucepan over medium heat. Add onion and cook, stirring, until softened, about 5 minutes. Add flour and cook, stirring constantly, 1 minute; gradually whisk in milk until smooth. Cook, stirring constantly, until sauce bubbles and thickens, about 4 minutes. Stir in Cheddar, salt, mustard powder, and pepper; cook, stirring, until cheese is melted, about 1 minute longer.

4 Remove saucepan from heat; stir in macaroni. Spoon into prepared baking dish. Sprinkle bread crumbs evenly over macaroni mixture; spray crumbs with nonstick spray. Bake until casserole is bubbly and top is golden, about 30 minutes.

PER SERVING (about 1 cup): 342 Cal, 6 g Fat, 3 g Sat Fat, 0 g Trans Fat, 15 mg Chol, 590 mg Sod, 54 g Carb, 5 g Fib, 20 g Prot, 281 mg Calc.

★ **FYI** ★ The macaroni and cheese can also be baked in four individual ovenproof baking cups. The baking time will be about 20 minutes.

PENNE WITH TOMATOES, RED ONION, AND BLUE CHEESE

SERVES 8

7 PointsPlus® value

PER SERVING

▲ 1 pound whole wheat penne

▲ 1 large red onion, chopped

▲ 1 cup halved cherry tomatoes

½ teaspoon salt

¼ teaspoon black pepper

¼ cup coarsely chopped fresh flat-leaf parsley

1 teaspoon dried thyme

1 cup crumbled reduced-fat blue cheese

1 Cook penne according to package directions, omitting salt if desired. Drain and keep warm.

2 Meanwhile, spray large nonstick skillet with nonstick spray and set over medium heat. Add onion and cook, stirring, until golden, about 8 minutes. Add tomatoes, salt, and pepper; cook until tomatoes are softened, about 4 minutes longer.

3 Transfer onion mixture to serving bowl. Add pasta and remaining ingredients. Toss until mixed well.

PER SERVING (about 1½ cups): 265 Cal, 5 g Total Fat, 2 g Sat Fat, 0 g Trans Fat, 10 mg Chol, 288 mg Sod, 46 g Carb, 4 g Sugar, 6 g Fib, 12 g Prot, 132 mg Calc.

★ **FYI** ★ To turn this flavorful pasta dish into a balanced full meal, serve it with a baby romaine lettuce and radicchio salad dressed with red wine vinegar and a pinch of salt and black pepper.

CREAMY CHEDDAR CHEESE SOUP

4 PointsPlus® value

PER SERVING

1 Heat oil in large nonstick saucepan over medium heat. Add onion, celery, and carrot; cook, stirring, until onion is softened, about 5 minutes. Stir in flour and mustard powder; cook, stirring, 1 minute. Stir in broth; simmer 15 minutes.

2 Puree soup, in batches, in blender or food processor. Return soup to saucepan and stir in evaporated milk; cook over medium heat until heated through, about 5 minutes (do not boil). Add Cheddar and Worcestershire sauce; cook, stirring, just until cheese is melted.

PER SERVING (about 1 cup): 175 Cal, 5 g Total Fat, 3 g Sat Fat, 0 g Trans Fat, 11 mg Chol, 381 mg Sod, 15 g Carb, 8 g Sugar, 1 g Fib, 17 g Prot, 339 mg Calc.

2 teaspoons olive oil

▲ 1 small onion, chopped

▲ 1 celery stalk, chopped

▲ 1 carrot, chopped

3 tablespoons all-purpose flour

¼ teaspoon mustard powder

▲ 1 (32-ounce) carton reduced-sodium chicken broth

1 (12-ounce) can fat-free evaporated milk

2 cups shredded reduced-fat yellow Cheddar cheese

2 teaspoons Worcestershire sauce

ALL AMERICAN

To make this soup New England style, use a Vermont Cheddar cheese, such as Cabot, Grafton, or Shelburne Farms, which are some of the finest Cheddar cheeses produced in America.

WILD MUSHROOM AND FETA CHEESE FRITTATA

SERVES 4

PER SERVING

- ▲ 4 large eggs
- ▲ 4 large egg whites
- ▲ ¼ cup fat-free milk
- ½ teaspoon salt
- ¼ teaspoon black pepper
- 2 teaspoons olive oil
- ▲ ¾ pound assorted mushrooms (such as white, oyster, cremini, and shiitake), sliced
- 3 shallots, thinly sliced
- ½ teaspoon dried thyme or herbes de Provence
- ▲ ½ cup crumbled fat-free feta cheese

1 Whisk together eggs, egg whites, milk, salt, and pepper in medium bowl.

2 Heat oil in 10-inch ovenproof skillet over medium heat. Add mushrooms, shallots, and thyme; cook, stirring, until mushrooms have released their juice and it is evaporated, about 8 minutes.

3 Preheat broiler.

4 Pour egg mixture over mushroom mixture. Cook, without stirring, until eggs are almost set, about 10 minutes. Sprinkle evenly with feta. Broil 5 inches from heat until cheese is softened, about 3 minutes. Cut into 4 wedges.

PER SERVING (1 wedge): 168 Cal, 7 g Total Fat, 2 g Sat Fat, 0 g Trans Fat, 217 mg Chol, 555 mg Sod, 10 g Carb, 3 g Sugar, 1 g Fib, 16 g Prot, 118 mg Calc.

★ **FYI** ★ The commercial cultivation of mushrooms began in 1896 in the Brandywine Valley outside of Philadelphia. The soil was ideal for growing a variety of mushrooms and this holds true today. If using shiitake mushrooms in this frittata, be sure to remove the stems, which are inedible.

TWICE-BAKED POTATOES WITH CRISPY PROSCIUTTO AND GOAT CHEESE

5 PointsPlus® value

PER SERVING

1 Preheat oven to 425°F.

2 Place potatoes directly on oven rack and bake until fork-tender, about 45 minutes. Transfer to wire rack and let cool slightly. Reduce oven temperature to 375°F.

3 Cut potatoes lengthwise in half. Scoop flesh into medium bowl, leaving ¼-inch shell in 4 of potato shells. Discard remaining 4 potato shells.

4 With potato masher, mash potatoes with milk, goat cheese, chives, and oil. Mound potato mixture evenly in potato shells. Sprinkle each stuffed potato with 1 tablespoon of prosciutto and transfer to baking sheet. Bake until potato mixture is heated through and topping is lightly browned, about 10 minutes.

- 4 (5-ounce) baking potatoes, scrubbed
- ⅓ cup fat-free milk

⅓ cup reduced-fat soft goat cheese, at room temperature

1 tablespoon snipped fresh chives

1 tablespoon extra-virgin olive oil

2 (½-ounce) slices prosciutto, crisp cooked and crumbled

PER SERVING (1 stuffed potato): 168 Cal, 5 g Total Fat, 1 g Sat Fat, 0 g Trans Fat, 6 mg Chol, 420 mg Sod, 27 g Carb, 4 g Sugar, 3 g Fib, 9 g Prot, 92 mg Calc.

★ **FYI** ★ Enjoy a special Sunday dinner by serving these classic potatoes with roasted beef tenderloin and steamed green beans. Three ounces of trimmed cooked beef tenderloin per serving will increase the *PointsPlus* value by **4.**

CLASSIC SCALLOPED POTATOES

1 Preheat oven to 425°F. Spray 2-quart baking dish or shallow casserole dish with nonstick spray.

2 Whisk together broth and flour in medium saucepan until smooth. Add milk, salt, pepper, and nutmeg, whisking until smooth. Bring sauce to boil, whisking constantly until slightly thickened; remove saucepan from heat.

3 Arrange half of potatoes in prepared baking dish, slightly overlapping slices. Sprinkle with ½ cup of Gruyère; arrange remaining potatoes on top. Pour white sauce evenly over potatoes.

4 Bake 25 minutes. Press down on potatoes with spatula to completely submerge potatoes in sauce; sprinkle with remaining ½ cup cheese. Bake until potatoes are tender and top is browned, about 20 minutes longer. Let stand about 20 minutes before serving.

- ½ cup reduced-sodium chicken broth
- 1 tablespoon all-purpose flour
- 2 cups low-fat (1%) milk
- 1 teaspoon salt
- ½ teaspoon black pepper
- ⅛ teaspoon ground nutmeg
- 2 pounds Yukon Gold potatoes, peeled and thinly sliced
- 1 cup shredded Gruyère cheese

PER SERVING (⅛ of potatoes): 180 Cal, 5 g Total Fat, 3 g Sat Fat, 0 g Trans Fat, 18 mg Chol, 371 mg Sod, 25 g Carb, 4 g Sugar, 2 g Fib, 8 g Prot, 219 mg Calc.

★ **FYI** ★ These scalloped potatoes can be baked up to 2 hours ahead. Cover with foil and set aside until about 30 minutes before serving time. Bake the gratin at 350°F until heated through, about 30 minutes.

MIXED GREENS WITH PECANS, GOAT CHEESE, AND DRIED CRANBERRIES

PER SERVING

1½ tablespoons water

1 tablespoon extra-virgin olive oil

1½ tablespoons red wine vinegar

½ teaspoon salt

¼ teaspoon black pepper

▲ 10 cups lightly packed mixed baby salad greens

¼ cup pecans, coarsely chopped and toasted

¼ cup dried cranberries

⅓ cup crumbled reduced-fat soft goat cheese

1 To make dressing, whisk together water, oil, vinegar, salt, and pepper in salad bowl.

2 Add salad greens, pecans, and cranberries to dressing; toss until mixed well. Top with goat cheese.

PER SERVING (about 1½ cups): 91 Cal, 6 g Total Fat, 1 g Sat Fat, 0 g Trans Fat, 0 mg Chol, 300 mg Sod, 10 g Carb, 6 g Sugar, 3 g Fib, 2 g Prot, 19 mg Calc.

★ **FYI** ★ To toast the pecans, preheat an oven or toaster oven to 350°F. Spread the pecans in a baking pan and toast, shaking the pan occasionally, until the pecans are crisp and lightly browned, 7–10 minutes.

MIXED GREENS WITH PECANS,
GOAT CHEESE, AND DRIED CRANBERRIES

WARM SPINACH, MUSHROOM, AND BACON SALAD

SERVES 6 | 20 MIN

- 1 (10-ounce) package baby spinach
- 12 large white mushrooms, sliced
- 1 small red onion, thinly sliced
- ¼ teaspoon black pepper
- ¼ cup cider vinegar
- 2 tablespoons honey
- 2 teaspoons Dijon mustard
- ⅓ cup crumbled reduced-fat blue cheese
- 3 slices turkey bacon, crisp cooked and crumbled

1 Toss together spinach, mushrooms, onion, and pepper in salad bowl.

2 To make dressing, combine vinegar, honey, and mustard in microwavable bowl. Microwave on High until hot, about 40 seconds; stir until mixed well.

3 Pour dressing over salad and toss until coated evenly. Sprinkle with blue cheese and bacon.

PER SERVING (⅙ of salad): 100 Cal, 3 g Total Fat, 1 g Sat Fat, 0 g Trans Fat, 11 mg Chol, 327 mg Sod, 15 g Carb, 7 g Sugar, 2 g Fib, 6 g Prot, 77 mg Calc.

★ **FYI** ★ To turn this classic salad into a main dish, add cooked peeled and deveined shrimp to the salad in step 3 (1½ pounds of cooked large shrimp will increase the per-serving *PointsPlus* value by **2**).

CHEDDAR-ROSEMARY BISCUITS

3
PointsPlus®
value

PER SERVING

1 Whisk together all-purpose flour, white whole wheat flour, baking powder, salt, and baking soda in large bowl. With pastry blender or 2 knives used scissor-fashion, cut in butter until mixture resembles coarse crumbs. Stir in Cheddar and rosemary. Gradually add buttermilk, stirring just until flour mixture is moistened.

2 Knead flour mixture in bowl a few times to form soft dough. Shape dough into disk; wrap in plastic wrap and refrigerate at least 15 minutes or up to several hours.

3 Preheat oven to 425°F. Spray large baking sheet with nonstick spray.

4 Lightly sprinkle work surface with flour. With floured rolling pin, roll out dough to scant ½-inch thickness. With floured 2-inch round cutter, cut out biscuits without twisting cutter. Gather scraps and reroll, making total of 12 biscuits. Place on prepared baking sheet.

5 Bake until biscuits are golden brown, 12–15 minutes. Serve hot or warm.

1¼ cups all-purpose flour

½ cup white whole wheat flour

1½ teaspoons baking powder

1 teaspoon salt

½ teaspoon baking soda

3 tablespoons cold unsalted butter, cut into pieces

½ cup finely shredded reduced-fat Cheddar cheese

2 teaspoons minced fresh rosemary

¾ cup low-fat buttermilk

PER SERVING (1 biscuit): 106 Cal, 4 g Total Fat, 2 g Sat Fat, 0 g Trans Fat, 9 mg Chol, 361 mg Sod, 15 g Carb, 1 g Sugar, 1 g Fib, 4 g Prot, 5 mg Calc.

★ **FYI** ★ To turn these biscuits into a substantial snack or light bite, split the biscuits while warm and fill with thin slices of lean ham. Two ounces of thinly sliced lean ham per serving will increase the **PointsPlus** value by **2**.

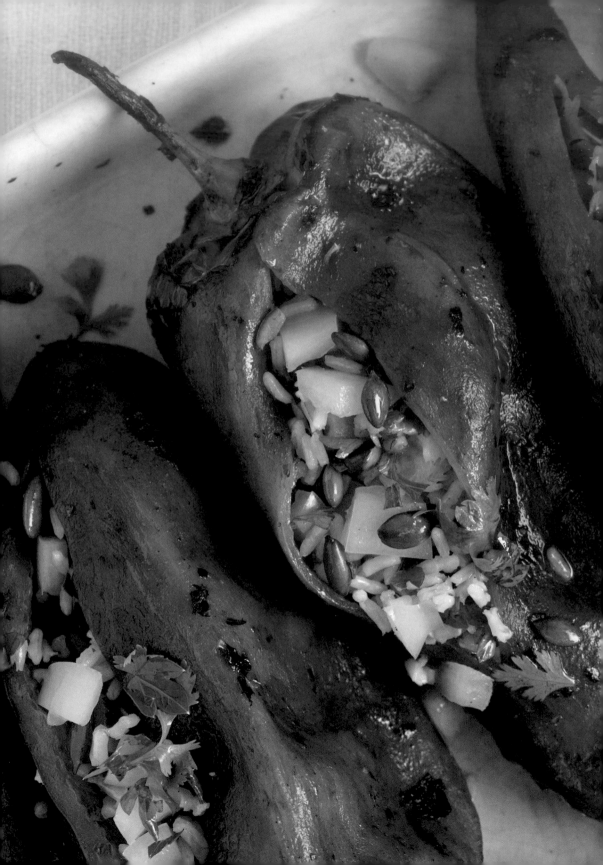

SPICY

CILANTRO RICE—STUFFED
POBLANOS, PAGE 87

★ MAIN DISHES ★

Slow-Cooker Chili Steak and Black Bean Tacos, 67

Steak on Garlic Bread with Tomato-Avocado Salsa, 68

Beef and Beer Chili, 70

All Peppered Up Cajun Jambalaya, 71

Grilled Tequila, Citrus, and Jalapeño Chicken, 72

Grilled Chicken and Poblano Posole, 74

Tongue Tingling Buffalo Chicken Tenders, 75

Five-Way Cincinnati Turkey-Cayenne Chili, 77

Smoky Pork BBQ on Buns, 78

Spicy Crab, Shrimp, and Cherry Tomato Gumbo, 80

Shrimp, Avocado, and Jalapeño Fajitas, 81

Pickled Shrimp and Potatoes, 83

Pasta with Shrimp Scampi, 84

Pasta with Red Clam Sauce Fra Diavolo, 86

★ SIDES ★

Cilantro Rice–Stuffed Poblanos, 87

Boston Baked Beans with Spicy Brown Mustard, 89

Cold Sesame Noodles, 90

Peppery Corn Sticks, 91

★ CONDIMENTS ★

Slow-Cooker Spiced Apple Butter, 92

Fresh and Fast Ginger-Peach Chutney, 93

SLOW-COOKER CHILI STEAK AND BLACK BEAN TACOS

8
PointsPlus®
value

PER SERVING

1 Mix together broth and chili powder in 5- or 6-quart slow cooker; add steak. Cover and cook until steak is fork-tender, 4–5 hours on high or 8–10 hours on low.

2 Transfer steak to cutting board; discard all but ¼ cup of cooking liquid. Wipe out slow cooker. With 2 forks, finely shred beef. Return beef to slow cooker; stir in reserved cooking liquid, the beans, and chiles. Cover and cook on high until heated through, about 5 minutes.

3 To assemble tacos, divide beef mixture evenly among tortillas. Top each taco with 1 tablespoon of salsa and 1 tablespoon of sour cream; sprinkle evenly with cilantro. Fold tortillas in half to enclose filling.

- 1½ cups reduced-sodium beef broth
- 1 tablespoon chili powder
- 1 (1-pound) flank steak, trimmed
- ¾ cup canned black beans, rinsed and drained
- 2 tablespoons canned chopped mild green chiles, drained
- 12 (6-inch) corn tortillas, warmed
- 12 tablespoons fat-free salsa
- 12 tablespoons fat-free sour cream
- ¼ cup lightly packed fresh cilantro leaves

PER SERVING (2 tacos): 318 Cal, 7 g Total Fat, 2 g Sat Fat, 0 g Trans Fat, 31 mg Chol, 405 mg Sod, 40 g Carb, 1 g Sugar, 4 g Fib, 22 g Prot, 67 mg Calc.

★ **FYI** ★ Serving the tacos with additional fat-free salsa will contribute even more flavor.

STEAK ON GARLIC BREAD WITH TOMATO-AVOCADO SALSA

SERVES 4 ....

PER SERVING

▲ 1 pint cherry tomatoes, quartered

½ Hass avocado, pitted, peeled, and diced

▲ ½ onion, thinly sliced

¼ cup chopped fresh cilantro

▲ 1 jalapeño pepper, seeded and minced

3 tablespoons cider vinegar

▲ 1 (1-pound) boneless sirloin steak, trimmed

1 teaspoon dried oregano

½ teaspoon salt

½ teaspoon black pepper

2 large garlic cloves, peeled and halved

4 (1½-ounce) slices whole wheat country-style bread, toasted

1 To make salsa, stir together tomatoes, avocado, onion, cilantro, jalapeño, and vinegar in medium bowl.

2 Spray broiler rack with nonstick spray and preheat broiler.

3 Sprinkle steak with oregano, salt, and black pepper. Place steak on prepared broiler rack and broil steak 5 inches from heat until instant-read thermometer inserted into side of steak registers 145°F for medium, about 5 minutes per side. Transfer to cutting board and let stand 5 minutes. Cut steak across grain into slices.

4 Rub cut side of garlic over one side of each slice of toasted bread. Top evenly with steak and salsa.

PER SERVING (1 open-face sandwich): 319 Cal, 9 g Total Fat, 3 g Sat Fat, 0 g Trans Fat, 49 mg Chol, 552 mg Sod, 26 g Carb, 6 g Sugar, 6 g Fib, 33 g Prot, 86 mg Calc.

....

★ **FYI** ★ To make this sandwich even more satisfying, top the bread with baby spinach leaves before adding the steak and salsa.

....

STEAK ON GARLIC BREAD WITH TOMATO-AVOCADO SALSA

BEEF AND BEER CHILI

SERVES 6

PER SERVING

2 tablespoons chili powder

2 teaspoons ground cumin

1 teaspoon dried oregano

½ teaspoon salt

¼ teaspoon black pepper

1 tablespoon canola oil

▲ 2 pounds sirloin or top round steak, trimmed and cut into ½-inch pieces

▲ 1 large onion, chopped

3 large garlic cloves, minced

1 (12-ounce) can light beer

▲ 1 (14 ½-ounce) can fire-roasted diced tomatoes

1 cup water

▲ 1 small red bell pepper, diced

▲ 1 small red onion, diced

1 Mix together chili powder, cumin, oregano, salt, and black pepper in cup.

2 Heat oil in Dutch oven over medium-high heat. Cook beef, in batches, until browned, transferring each batch to medium bowl as it is browned. Reduce heat to medium. Add chopped onion to pot and cook, stirring, until softened, about 5 minutes. Add garlic and cook, stirring, until fragrant, about 1 minute. Sprinkle spice mixture over onion mixture; cook, stirring, until fragrant, about 1 minute longer.

3 Pour beer over onion mixture and cook, stirring to scrape up any browned bits from bottom of pot. Return beef to pot along with tomatoes and water; bring to boil. Reduce heat and simmer, covered, stirring occasionally, until meat is very tender, about 1½ hours.

4 Serve chili accompanied by bowls of bell pepper and red onion.

PER SERVING (1 cup): 293 Cal, 9 g Total Fat, 3 g Sat Fat, 0 g Trans Fat, 66 mg Chol, 453 mg Sod, 11 g Carb, 5 g Sugar, 3 g Fib, 37 g Prot, 64 mg Calc.

★ **FYI** ★ Serve the chili along with a bowl of brown rice (⅔ cup cooked brown rice per serving will increase the **PointsPlus** value by **3**).

ALL PEPPERED UP CAJUN JAMBALAYA

11 PointsPlus© value

PER SERVING

1 Heat oil in large nonstick skillet over medium-high heat. Add chicken and cook until browned on all sides, about 5 minutes. Transfer to plate.

2 Add bell peppers, onion, celery, and garlic to skillet; cook, stirring, until softened, about 5 minutes. Stir in rice, broth, tomatoes, thyme, black pepper, salt, cayenne, and bay leaf; bring to boil. Reduce heat and simmer, covered, 20 minutes.

3 Return chicken to skillet and simmer, covered, 5 minutes. Add shrimp and cook, covered, until shrimp are just opaque in center, chicken is cooked through, and rice is tender, about 5 minutes longer. Remove bay leaf.

PER SERVING (about 2 cups): 422 Cal, 7 g Total Fat, 1 g Sat Fat, 0 g Trans Fat, 147 mg Chol, 614 mg Sod, 50 g Carb, 8 g Sugar, 3 g Fib, 40 g Prot, 92 mg Calc.

- 2 teaspoons canola oil
- 1 pound skinless boneless chicken breasts, cut into 1-inch chunks
- 2 green bell peppers, chopped
- 1 onion, sliced
- 2 celery stalks, sliced
- 3 large garlic cloves, minced
- 1 cup long-grain white rice
- 3 cups reduced-sodium chicken broth
- 1 (14 ½-ounce) can diced tomatoes, drained
- 2 teaspoons dried thyme
- ½ teaspoon black pepper
- ¼ teaspoon salt
- ¼–½ teaspoon cayenne
- 1 bay leaf
- ½ pound large shrimp, peeled and deveined

★ **FYI** ★ In Cajun cooking, many dishes begin with the "holy trinity" of sautéed onion, green bell pepper, and celery.

GRILLED TEQUILA, CITRUS, AND JALAPEÑO CHICKEN

SERVES 4

6 PointsPlus® value

PER SERVING

¼ cup lime juice

¼ cup orange juice

¼ cup tequila

▲ 1 jalapeño pepper, seeded and minced

2 large garlic cloves, minced

1 tablespoon canola oil

½ teaspoon salt

¼ teaspoon black pepper

▲ 4 (5-ounce) skinless boneless chicken breasts

1   Combine all ingredients except chicken in large zip-close plastic bag; add chicken. Squeeze out air and seal bag; turn to coat chicken. Refrigerate, turning bag occasionally, at least 20 minutes or up to 4 hours.

2   Spray grill rack with nonstick spray. Preheat grill to medium or prepare medium fire.

3   Place chicken on prepared grill rack and grill until cooked through, about 5 minutes per side.

PER SERVING (1 chicken breast): 231 Cal, 7 g Total Fat, 1 g Sat Fat, 0 g Trans Fat, 78 mg Chol, 360 mg Sod, 4 g Carb, 0 g Sugar, 0 g Fib, 29 g Prot, 21 mg Calc.

★ **FYI** ★   To make this chicken even more enjoyable, serve it with grilled corn on the cob. One medium ear of corn per serving will increase the *PointsPlus* value by *2*.

GRILLED TEQUILA, CITRUS, AND JALAPEÑO
CHICKEN WITH CUCUMBER-DILL SALAD WITH
SOUR CREAM DRESSING, PAGE 114

GRILLED CHICKEN AND POBLANO POSOLE

7
PointsPlus®
value

PER SERVING

SERVES 6

- ▲ 1 pound skinless boneless chicken breasts
- ¾ teaspoon salt
- ½ teaspoon black pepper
- ▲ 6 poblano peppers
- 1 tablespoon canola oil
- ▲ 1 red onion, chopped
- 2 large garlic cloves, minced
- 2 teaspoons ground cumin
- 1 teaspoon dried oregano
- ▲ 3 (14½-ounce) cans reduced-sodium chicken broth
- ▲ 1 (19-ounce) can hominy
- Juice of ½ lime
- ½ Hass avocado, pitted, peeled, and diced
- ▲ 6 large radishes, thinly sliced
- Coarsely chopped fresh cilantro

1 Spray grill rack with nonstick spray. Preheat grill to medium or prepare medium fire.

2 Sprinkle chicken with ½ teaspoon of salt and ¼ teaspoon of black pepper. Spray chicken with nonstick spray. Place chicken and poblano peppers on grill rack and grill, turning, until chicken is cooked through and peppers are charred on all sides, about 10 minutes. Transfer chicken and poblanos to cutting board.

3 When cool enough to handle, with your fingers, coarsely shred chicken. Peel and seed peppers and coarsely chop.

4 Heat oil in Dutch oven over medium heat. Add onion and cook, stirring, until softened, about 5 minutes. Add garlic, cumin, and oregano; cook, stirring, until fragrant, about 1 minute. Stir in broth, hominy, and remaining ¼ teaspoon salt and ¼ teaspoon black pepper; cook, stirring, until slightly reduced, about 30 minutes. Add chicken, poblanos, and lime juice to Dutch oven; cook until heated through, about 3 minutes. Ladle stew evenly among 6 soup bowls. Top each serving with one-sixth of avocado and radishes and sprinkle with cilantro.

PER SERVING (about 1 cup): 281 Cal, 10 g Total Fat, 2 g Sat Fat, 0 g Trans Fat, 42 mg Chol, 588 mg Sod, 28 g Carb, 3 g Sugar, 7 g Fib, 23 g Prot, 52 mg Calc.

★ **FYI** ★ Posole is a thick soup of Mexican origin whose main ingredient is hominy, dried white or yellow corn kernels. This satisfying soup is a mainstay in New Mexico and is popular at Christmas time and New Year's Day. Hominy is sold dried or canned.

TONGUE TINGLING BUFFALO CHICKEN TENDERS

5 PointsPlus© value

PER SERVING

SERVES 6

1   Spray broiler rack with nonstick spray. Preheat broiler.

2   Toss together chicken, butter, and pepper sauce in medium bowl until coated evenly. Arrange chicken on prepared rack. Broil 5 inches from heat until cooked through, about 4 minutes per side. Pile chicken onto serving plate.

3   To make sauce, whisk together blue cheese dressing and milk in serving bowl. Serve with chicken and celery.

▲ **1¼ pounds chicken tenders, cut lengthwise into ½-inch-wide strips**

2 tablespoons unsalted butter, melted

2 tablespoons hot pepper sauce (such as Frank's)

⅔ cup reduced-fat blue cheese dressing

▲ **¼ cup fat-free milk**

▲ **12 celery stalks, cut into sticks**

PER SERVING (⅙ of chicken, about 3 tablespoons dressing, and 2 celery stalks): 211 Cal, 8 g Total Fat, 3 g Sat Fat, 0 g Trans Fat, 73 mg Chol, 500 mg Sod, 9 g Carb, 4 g Sugar, 1 g Fib, 23 g Prot, 52 mg Calc.

ALL AMERICAN

Buffalo Chicken was created at the Anchor Bar in Buffalo, New York in the early 1960s as a way to use up a surplus of chicken wings. The chef deep-fried the wings, tossed them in a mixture of melted margarine and hot sauce, and served them with blue cheese dressing as a way to cut the heat.

FIVE-WAY CINCINNATI TURKEY-CAYENNE CHILI

11
PointsPlus®
value

PER SERVING

SERVES 6

1 Heat oil in Dutch oven over medium heat. Add onion and garlic; cook, stirring, until onion is softened, about 5 minutes. Add turkey and cook, breaking it up with side of spoon, until no longer pink, about 5 minutes. Stir in chili powder, paprika, cinnamon, cumin, salt, and cayenne; cook, stirring, until fragrant, about 1 minute longer.

2 Stir beans, tomatoes, water, and vinegar into Dutch oven; cook, stirring occasionally, until chili is slightly thickened, about 30 minutes.

3 Meanwhile, cook spaghetti according to package directions, omitting salt if desired. Drain. Divide spaghetti evenly among 6 large shallow bowls. Top evenly with chili and sprinkle 2 tablespoons Cheddar over each serving. Serve with scallions.

PER SERVING (1 cup spaghetti and about 1½ cups chili): 446 Cal, 6 g Total Fat, 1 g Sat Fat, 0 g Trans Fat, 33 mg Chol, 498 mg Sod, 66 g Carb, 7 g Sugar, 16 g Fib, 37 g Prot, 111 mg Calc.

1 tablespoon olive oil

▲ 1 large onion, chopped

2 large garlic cloves, minced

▲ 1 pound ground skinless turkey breast

1 tablespoon chili powder

1 tablespoon paprika

¾ teaspoon ground cinnamon

½ teaspoon ground cumin

½ teaspoon salt

¼ teaspoon cayenne

▲ 1 (15 ½-ounce) can red kidney beans, rinsed and drained

▲ 1 (14 ½-ounce) can diced tomatoes with green chiles

1 cup water

2 teaspoons cider vinegar

▲ 12 ounces whole wheat spaghetti

12 tablespoons shredded reduced-fat Cheddar cheese

▲ 2 scallions, sliced

ALL AMERICAN

In Cincinnati, the question isn't *if* you want chili but *how* you want it. Three-way chili is chili served over spaghetti and topped with a generous amount of Cheddar cheese, four-way chili contains onions, and five-way chili also contains beans.

SMOKY PORK BBQ ON BUNS

SERVES 6

PER SERVING

3 tablespoons packed brown sugar

2 teaspoons smoked paprika

2 teaspoons chili powder

1½ teaspoons ground cumin

¾ teaspoon salt

¾ teaspoon black pepper

▲ 1 (1½-pound) lean pork tenderloin

1 tablespoon canola oil

⅔ cup cider vinegar

⅓ cup water

¼ cup ketchup

▲ 2 tablespoons minced onion

1 garlic clove, minced

¼ teaspoon red pepper flakes

6 whole wheat hamburger buns, split and toasted

1 Preheat oven to 450°F. Spray medium roasting pan with nonstick spray.

2 Mix together 1 tablespoon of brown sugar, the paprika, chili powder, cumin, ½ teaspoon of salt, and ½ teaspoon of black pepper in cup. Sprinkle spice mixture all over pork, pressing so it adheres.

3 Heat oil in large nonstick skillet over medium-high heat. Add pork and cook until browned on all sides, about 5 minutes. Transfer to prepared roasting pan. Roast until instant-read thermometer inserted into center of meat registers 145°F for medium, about 15 minutes. Transfer to cutting board and let stand 10 minutes.

4 Meanwhile, combine vinegar, water, ketchup, onion, remaining 2 tablespoons brown sugar, ¼ teaspoon salt, ¼ teaspoon black pepper, and the pepper flakes in small saucepan and bring to boil. Reduce heat and cook until reduced to ¾ cup, about 15 minutes.

5 Slice pork across grain. Divide pork evenly among bottoms of buns. Drizzle with about ¼ cup of sauce. Cover with tops of buns. Serve remaining ½ cup sauce alongside.

PER SERVING (1 sandwich): 314 Cal, 7 g Total Fat, 1 g Sat Fat, 0 g Trans Fat, 74 mg Chol, 681 mg Sod, 35 g Carb, 11 g Sugar, 4 g Fib, 28 g Prot, 72 mg Calc.

★ **FYI** ★ Serve the barbecue sandwiches with a side of coleslaw. Dress packaged coleslaw mix with cider vinegar and a pinch each of salt and pepper. If desired, top each sandwich with a little of the coleslaw.

SPICY CRAB, SHRIMP, AND CHERRY TOMATO GUMBO

SERVES 4

PER SERVING

2 tablespoons canola oil

2 tablespoons all-purpose flour

▲ 1 red onion, chopped

▲ 1 green bell pepper, chopped

▲ 2 celery stalks, chopped

2 large garlic cloves, minced

▲ 3 cups reduced-sodium chicken broth

▲ 1 (10-ounce) package frozen whole okra

▲ 1 cup halved cherry tomatoes

2 teaspoons hot pepper sauce or to taste

½ teaspoon dried oregano

1 bay leaf

▲ ½ pound peeled and deveined large shrimp

▲ ½ pound lump crabmeat, picked over

▲ 2 cups hot cooked brown rice

▲ ⅓ cup thinly sliced scallions

1 To make roux, heat oil in Dutch oven over medium-low heat. Gradually stir in flour and cook, stirring constantly, until roux is deep brown (do not let burn), about 10 minutes. Add onion, bell pepper, and celery; cook, stirring, until softened, about 5 minutes. Add garlic and cook, stirring, until fragrant, about 1 minute longer.

2 Gradually stir in broth and bring to boil. Reduce heat and add okra, tomatoes, pepper sauce, oregano, and bay leaf; simmer, covered, 15 minutes. Add shrimp and crabmeat; cook until shrimp are opaque in center, about 3 minutes longer. Remove bay leaf and discard.

3 Divide rice evenly among 4 large shallow bowls. Ladle gumbo evenly on top and sprinkle with scallions.

PER SERVING (½ cup rice and about 1½ cups gumbo): 363 Cal, 10 g Total Fat, 1 g Sat Fat, 0 g Trans Fat, 124 mg Chol, 457 mg Sod, 40 g Carb, 6 g Sugar, 6 g Fib, 30 g Prot, 176 mg Calc.

ALL AMERICAN

Gumbo, which is a derivation of the African word for okra, is a spicy stewlike dish that is a mainstay in New Orleans. It varies from cook to cook, but they all start with the same base: a rich tasting dark brown roux (flour and fat). According to gumbo experts, the key to a great gumbo is cooking the roux very slowly.

SHRIMP, AVOCADO, AND JALAPEÑO FAJITAS

PointsPlus© value

PER SERVING

1 Combine jalapeño, lemon zest and juice, garlic, chile powder, cumin, and pepper sauce in large zip-close plastic bag; add shrimp. Squeeze out air and seal bag; turn to coat shrimp. Refrigerate, turning bag occasionally, about 20 minutes.

2 Meanwhile, preheat oven or toaster oven to 400°F. Wrap tortillas in foil. Place in oven until warmed, about 10 minutes.

3 Spray large nonstick skillet with nonstick spray and set over medium-high heat. Remove shrimp from marinade; discard marinade. Add shrimp to skillet and cook, turning, until opaque in center, about 4 minutes.

4 Put shrimp, tomato, avocado, and cilantro in separate bowls. Stack tortillas on plate and cover with napkin to keep warm. Have diners assemble their own fajitas by placing one-eighth of shrimp along center of each warm tortilla, then topping each with one-eighth of tomato and avocado; sprinkle with cilantro.

PER SERVING (2 fajitas): 203 Cal, 5 g Total Fat, 1 g Sat Fat, 0 g Trans Fat, 84 mg Chol, 415 mg Sod, 28 g Carb, 3 g Sugar, 5 g Fib, 14 g Prot, 122 mg Calc.

- 1 jalapeño pepper, seeded and minced

  Grated zest of 1 lemon

  3 tablespoons lemon juice

  2 garlic cloves, minced

  1½ teaspoons chipotle chile powder

  1 teaspoon ground cumin

  Few drops hot pepper sauce or to taste

- 1 pound medium shrimp, peeled and deveined

  8 (8-inch) reduced-fat whole wheat tortillas

- 1 large tomato, seeded and diced

  1 small Hass avocado, pitted, peeled, and diced

  ¼ cup coarsely chopped fresh cilantro

★ **FYI** ★ Serve the fajitas with fat-free salsa and fat-free sour cream (¼ cup fat-free sour cream per serving will increase the **PointsPlus** value by **1**).

TURN UP THE HEAT WITH CHILES

Whether fresh, ground, dried, or bottled as sauce, chiles add punch to all manner of foods. Chile peppers can be mild, sweet, hot, or downright searingly hot. There are over 90 fresh and dried chiles, from the always-dependable jalapeño to the small and fiery Thai chile.

★ BUYING AND HANDLING FRESH CHILES ★

Chiles are green in their unripened state. When ripened and fully mature, they turn an array of colors from red to orange to yellow to purple. Always choose firm peppers without any wrinkles. At home, wrap them in paper towels and place them in the crisper drawer of the refrigerator, where they should keep for about 2 weeks. Chiles contain capsaicin, an active ingredient that causes a serious burning sensation when it comes in contact with skin. It is recommended to wear rubber gloves when working with chiles and to avoid touching your eyes. Here's how to prepare chiles before slicing, mincing, or chopping them: Cut off the stem end, then slice the chiles lengthwise in half. With the tip of the knife scrape out all the seeds and remove the ribs.

NAME	DESCRIPTION	BEST USES
Habaneros	and their close cousin Scotch bonnet peppers range from green to orange to red. They are lantern-shaped and about 2 inches long and almost as wide. The hottest chile grown in Central America and the Caribbean, they are up to 50 times hotter than a jalapeño!	salsas, sauces, chutneys, seafood marinades
Jalapeños	named after Jalapa the capitol of Veracruz, vary in color from bright to dark green to red. They are about 3 inches long and about 1 inch wide. It is the best known and most widely used chile in the U.S. Only a moderate amount of heat makes it welcome to most palates. When dried and smoked, jalapeños become the smoky, almost chocolate-flavored chipotle. When canned in a spicy tomato adobo sauce, they are called chipotles en adobo and are found in small cans in the Mexican food aisle of supermarkets.	salsas, sauces, guacamole, marinades, soups, stews, tamales, pickles, drinks
Poblanos	are tapered peppers about 4 inches long and 3 inches in diameter. They are thick-fleshed and range in heat from moderate to hot. Used extensively in Mexican cooking, poblanos are usually eaten roasted or grilled—never raw.	chiles rellenos and other stuffed vegetable dishes, sauces, moles
Serranos	are the most widely available hot chile in the U.S. These slender red or green tapered chiles range from 1 to 2 inches in length and are about ½ inch around. They are thick-fleshed and have a biting heat. In Mexico serranos are the preferred chile for salsa and are often pickled.	salsas, guacamole
Thai	are tiny—about 1 inch long and ¼ inch across—and have a very hot, lingering heat and an overabundance of seeds. They are usually bright green but can also be red. Thai chiles are highly regarded in Southeast Asian cooking.	noodle dishes, green papaya salad and other salads, sauces, soups

PICKLED SHRIMP AND POTATOES

PER SERVING

1 Combine lemon juice, vinegar, oil, dill sprigs, lemon, pickling spices, and sugar in large zip-close plastic bag; add shrimp. Squeeze out air and seal bag; turn to coat shrimp. Refrigerate, turning bag occasionally, at least 4 hours or up to overnight.

2 Remove shrimp from marinade; discard marinade. Toss together shrimp, potatoes, onion, bell pepper, and snipped dill in large bowl.

3 Divide frisée evenly among 4 plates. Top evenly with shrimp mixture.

PER SERVING (1 plate): 246 Cal, 8 g Total Fat, 1 g Sat Fat, 0 g Trans Fat, 168 mg Chol, 219 mg Sod, 22 g Carb, 4 g Sugar, 5 g Fib, 21 g Prot, 115 mg Calc.

⅓ cup lemon juice

¼ cup white vinegar

2 tablespoons canola oil

2 fresh dill sprigs + 2 tablespoons snipped fresh dill

1 lemon, sliced

1 tablespoon pickling spices, tied in cheesecloth

1 teaspoon sugar

▲ 1 pound cooked peeled and deveined large shrimp

▲ ¾ pound small red potatoes, cooked, and quartered

▲ ½ cup finely chopped red onion

▲ ½ red bell pepper, finely chopped

▲ 6 cups lightly packed torn frisée or escarole

★ **FYI** ★ Pickling spices is a mix of spices used to make pickles and pickled foods. The blend often contains bay leaves, cardamom, cinnamon, cloves, coriander, ginger, mustard seeds, and peppercorns. Jars of pickling spices can be found in the spice aisle in supermarkets.

PASTA WITH SHRIMP SCAMPI

SERVES 6

8 PointsPlus® value

PER SERVING

- ▲ 12 ounces whole wheat capellini or thin spaghetti

- 3 large garlic cloves, minced

- ▲ 1 pound medium shrimp, peeled and deveined

- 1 (8-ounce) bottle clam juice

- ½ cup dry white wine

- ½ teaspoon dried oregano

- ½ teaspoon salt

- ¼ teaspoon red pepper flakes

- ¼ cup chopped fresh flat-leaf parsley

- Grated zest of ½ lemon

- 1 tablespoon extra-virgin olive oil

- Lemon wedges

1 Cook pasta according to package direction, omitting salt if desired. Drain and transfer to serving bowl; keep pasta warm.

2 Meanwhile, spray large nonstick skillet with nonstick spray and set over medium heat. Add garlic and cook, stirring, until golden, about 2 minutes. Add shrimp, clam juice, wine, oregano, salt, and pepper flakes. Bring to simmer and cook until shrimp are opaque in center, about 3 minutes.

3 Add shrimp mixture, parsley, lemon zest, and oil to pasta; toss. Serve with lemon wedges.

PER SERVING (1 cup pasta, about 5 shrimp, and ¼ cup sauce): 295 Cal, 4 g Total Fat, 1 g Sat Fat, 0 g Trans Fat, 113 mg Chol, 410 mg Sod, 44 g Carb, 2 g Sugar, 7 g Fib, 21 g Prot, 59 mg Calc.

★ **FYI** ★ Here's how to clean shrimp easily and quickly: Starting at the head end, peel off the shell including the tail, if desired. Then, using a small knife, make a cut along the back of each shrimp to expose the black vein and pull it out.

PASTA WITH SHRIMP SCAMPI

PASTA WITH RED CLAM SAUCE FRA DIAVOLO

SERVES 4

PER SERVING

▲ 12 cherrystone clams, scrubbed

¼ cup dry white wine

3 large garlic cloves, minced

1 teaspoon dried oregano

¼ teaspoon red pepper flakes

▲ 8 ounces whole grain spaghetti

4 teaspoons olive oil

▲ 8 plum tomatoes, chopped

½ teaspoon salt

2 tablespoons chopped fresh basil

2 tablespoons chopped fresh flat-leaf parsley

1 Combine clams, wine, garlic, oregano, and pepper flakes in large saucepan over medium heat. Cook, covered, until clams open, about 5 minutes. With slotted spoon, transfer clams to medium bowl; reserve clam cooking liquid. Discard any clams that do not open. When cool enough to handle, remove clams and discard shells. Coarsely chop clams.

2 Cook spaghetti according to package directions, omitting salt if desired. Drain and transfer to serving bowl; keep warm.

3 Meanwhile, heat oil in medium nonstick skillet over medium heat. Add tomatoes and salt; cook, stirring occasionally, until tomatoes are softened, about 5 minutes. Stir in reserved clam cooking liquid; reduce heat and simmer until slightly reduced, about 5 minutes. Stir in clams and basil; cook just until clams are heated through, about 2 minutes. Pour sauce over pasta and toss until coated well. Sprinkle with parsley.

PER SERVING (1 cup pasta and about ¼ cup sauce): 319 Cal, 6 g Total Fat, 1 g Sat Fat, 0 g Trans Fat, 19 mg Chol, 332 mg Sod, 50 g Carb, 5 g Sugar, 9 g Fib, 17 g Prot, 74 mg Calc.

★ **FYI** ★ To start the meal, serve a tri-colored salad of thinly sliced radicchio, baby arugula, and thinly sliced Belgian endive dressed with balsamic vinegar and a sprinkling of salt and pepper.

CILANTRO RICE-STUFFED POBLANOS

PER SERVING

1 Cook rice according to package directions, omitting salt if desired.

2 Meanwhile, with knife, cut 2-inch-long lengthwise slit in each poblano, leaving stem intact. Carefully remove seeds and discard.

3 Stir together rice and remaining ingredients in medium bowl. Stuff each poblano with about ⅓ cup of rice mixture. Serve warm or at room temperature.

PER SERVING (2 stuffed peppers): 208 Cal, 9 g Total Fat, 1 g Sat Fat, 0 g Trans Fat, 0 mg Chol, 607 mg Sod, 31 g Carb, 1 g Sugar, 9 g Fib, 7 g Prot, 37 mg Calc.

- ⅔ cup brown or white rice
- 8 poblano peppers, roasted and peeled
- ½ yellow or red bell pepper, chopped

¼ cup chopped fresh cilantro

2 tablespoons pumpkin seeds, toasted and chopped

1 tablespoon olive oil

1 teaspoon ground cumin

1 teaspoon chili powder

1 teaspoon salt

★ **FYI** ★ You can roast the poblano peppers on a grill, under a broiler, or over a gas flame. Just be sure to roast them until blackened all over, then when cool enough to handle, remove all the skin and discard.

BOSTON BAKED BEANS
WITH SPICY BROWN MUSTARD

BOSTON BAKED BEANS WITH SPICY BROWN MUSTARD

4 PointsPlus® value
PER SERVING

1 To soak beans, combine beans with enough water to cover by 2 inches in large saucepan and bring to boil. Reduce heat and simmer 2 minutes. Remove saucepan from heat. Let stand, covered, 1 hour.

2 Drain beans and return to saucepan. Add enough water to cover by 3 inches and bring to boil. Reduce heat and simmer, covered, until beans are tender, about 40 minutes. Drain.

3 Preheat oven to 350°F.

4 Chop 4 slices of bacon. Combine beans, onion, and chopped bacon in deep 3-quart casserole dish or Dutch oven. Add remaining ingredients to bean mixture, stirring until mixed well. Place remaining 4 slices of bacon over bean mixture. Bake until sauce is thickened and beans are tender, about 2 hours.

- 1 pound dried navy or great northern beans, picked over
- 8 slices turkey bacon
- 1 large onion, chopped
- 3 cups water
- ⅓ cup pure maple syrup
- ½ cup ketchup
- 3 tablespoons light (mild) molasses
- ¼ cup spicy brown mustard
- ¼ teaspoon black pepper

PER SERVING (about ½ cup): 153 Cal, 2 g Total Fat, 1 g Sat Fat, 0 g Trans Fat, 7 mg Chol, 287 mg Sod, 25 g Carb, 9 g Sugar, 5 g Fib, 8 g Prot, 69 mg Calc.

★ **FYI** ★ Enjoy the baked beans with grilled trimmed boneless pork loin chops and coleslaw dressed with apple vinegar. A grilled 3-ounce pork chop per serving will increase the **PointsPlus** value by **3**.

COLD SESAME NOODLES

SERVES 6 ....

▲ 8 ounces whole wheat capellini

1½ tablespoons soy sauce

1½ tablespoons red wine vinegar

1 tablespoon Asian (dark) sesame oil

¼ teaspoon sugar

¼ teaspoon salt

⅛–¼ teaspoon red pepper flakes

▲ 1 small cucumber, peeled, seeded, and cut into thin matchsticks

▲ 1 small red bell pepper, cut into thin matchsticks

▲ 6 large radishes, cut into thin matchsticks

▲ 2 scallions, thinly sliced on diagonal

1 tablespoon sesame seeds, preferably black

1 Cook capellini according to package directions, omitting salt if desired. Drain and rinse under cool running water. Drain again.

2 Whisk together soy sauce, vinegar, oil, sugar, salt, and pepper flakes in serving bowl. Add pasta and toss until coated well. Add cucumber, bell pepper, radishes, and scallions; toss until mixed well. Serve sprinkled with sesame seeds.

PER SERVING (about 1⅓ cups): 174 Cal, 3 g Total Fat, 1 g Sat Fat, 0 g Trans Fat, 0 mg Chol, 242 mg Sod, 31 g Carb, 3 g Sugar, 6 g Fib, 7 g Prot, 31 mg Calc.

PEPPERY CORN STICKS

PER SERVING

1 Preheat oven to 450°F. Spray 7-mold corn stick pan with nonstick spray and place in oven to preheat.

2 Whisk together cornmeal, flour, sugar, baking powder, baking soda, salt, and pepper in medium bowl. Whisk together buttermilk, egg, and oil in small bowl. Add buttermilk mixture to cornmeal mixture, stirring just until cornmeal mixture is moistened (batter will be lumpy).

3 Wearing oven mitts, remove pan from oven. Divide half of batter among prepared molds, filling each about two-thirds full. Bake until tops of corn sticks spring back when lightly pressed, 8–10 minutes. Run tip of thin knife around edges of molds to help release corn sticks. Turn out onto wire rack.

4 Spray pan with nonstick spray. Repeat with remaining batter. Serve corn sticks warm or at room temperature.

1 cup cornmeal, preferably stone ground

½ cup white whole wheat flour

1 tablespoon sugar

½ teaspoon baking powder

½ teaspoon baking soda

½ teaspoon salt

¼–½ teaspoon black pepper

1 cup low-fat buttermilk

▲ 1 large egg

1 tablespoon canola oil

PER SERVING (2 corn sticks): 145 Cal, 4 g Total Fat, 1 g Sat Fat, 0 g Trans Fat, 32 mg Chol, 347 mg Sod, 23 g Carb, 3 g sugar, 4 g Fib, 4 g Prot, 57 mg Calc.

★ **FYI** ★ If you don't have a corn stick pan, make corn muffins by dividing the batter among 12 greased regular muffin cups. Reduce the oven temperature to 400°F and increase the baking time to about 20 minutes, or until a toothpick inserted into a muffin comes out clean.

SLOW-COOKER
SPICED APPLE BUTTER

SERVES 16 (makes 1½ cups)

▲ 3 Granny Smith apples, peeled, cored, and coarsely chopped

▲ 3 McIntosh apples, peeled, cored, and coarsely chopped

1 (6-ounce) can frozen apple juice concentrate, thawed

2 tablespoons pure maple syrup

1 tablespoon lemon juice

½ teaspoon ground cinnamon

¼ teaspoon ground allspice

1 Finely chop apples, in batches if necessary, in food processor; transfer to 5- or 6-quart slow cooker. Stir in apple juice concentrate. Cover and cook until mixture is very thick, 4–6 hours on high or 8–10 hours on low.

2 Stir in remaining ingredients until mixed well. Transfer apple butter to covered glass jars and refrigerate up to 2 weeks or freeze up to 6 months.

PER SERVING (2 tablespoons): 64 Cal, 0 g Total Fat, 0 g Sat Fat, 0 g Trans Fat, 0 mg Chol, 0 mg Sod, 17 g Carb, 14 g Sugar, 1 g Fib, 0 g Prot, 7 mg Calc.

★ **FYI** ★ Fresh pears or a combination of pears and apples can also be used for the fruit butter.

FRESH AND FAST
GINGER-PEACH CHUTNEY

PER SERVING

Toss together peaches and lemon juice in large bowl. Combine remaining ingredients in large saucepan and bring to boil. Reduce heat and simmer 5 minutes. Stir in peaches and bring to boil. Reduce heat and simmer 1 minute; let cool. Transfer chutney to covered glass jars and refrigerate up to 1 week.

PER SERVING (about ¼ cup): 70 Cal, 0 g Total Fat, 0 g Sat Fat, 0 g Trans Fat, 0 mg Chol, 73 mg Sod, 19 g Carb, 15 g Sugar, 1 g Fib, 1 g Prot, 6 mg Calc.

▲ 6 large firm-ripe peaches, peeled, pitted, and cut into ½-inch dice

2 tablespoons lemon juice

¾ cup dried cranberries

⅔ cup sugar

½ cup cider vinegar

2 tablespoons finely chopped shallot

2 teaspoons grated peeled fresh ginger

½ teaspoon salt

★ **FYI** ★ This summery chutney pairs well with shrimp or chicken. Four ounces of grilled shrimp per serving will increase the **PointsPlus** value by **2**, while a grilled 3-ounce skinless boneless chicken breast per serving will increase the **PointsPlus** value by **3.**

CREAMY

CREAMED CORN,
PAGE 116

★ LIGHT BITES ★

Kicked-Up Guacamole, 97

Classic Deviled Eggs, 98

Layered Refried Bean Dip, 100

★ SOUPS ★

Little Havana–Style Black Bean Soup, 101

Yellow Split Pea Soup, 103

Autumn Squash, Apple, and Mushroom Soup, 104

Peanut Soup, 105

She-Crab Soup, 106

New England–Style Wild Salmon Chowder, 108

Smoky New England Clam Chowder, 109

★ SIDES ★

Red, White, and Blue Potato Salad, 111

Pasta Salad with Lemon Mayonnaise, 112

Cucumber-Dill Salad with Sour Cream Dressing, 114

Mashed Potatoes with Roasted Garlic, 115

Creamed Corn, 116

Fresh Corn and Chive Spoon Bread, 117

Cabbage in Caraway–Sour Cream Sauce, 118

Creamy Spinach with Parmesan, 119

KICKED-UP GUACAMOLE

20 MIN   S E R V E S   8

Coarsely mash avocados in medium bowl. Add remaining ingredients and gently stir until combined. If not serving right way, press piece of plastic wrap directly onto surface to prevent guacamole from browning. Refrigerate up to 4 hours.

PER SERVING (¼ cup): 59 Cal, 5 g Total Fat, 1 g Sat Fat, 0 g Trans Fat, 0 mg Chol, 148 mg Sod, 4 g Carb, 0 g Sugar, 2 g Fib, 1 g Prot, 7 mg Calc.

2 Hass avocados, halved, pitted, and peeled

3 tablespoons chopped fresh cilantro

▲ 1 scallion, chopped

▲ 1 small jalapeño pepper, seeded and minced

2 tablespoons lime juice

½ teaspoon salt

★ **FYI** ★ Guacamole tastes best when freshly made. If you want to get a head start, mix together everything but the avocado and set it aside for up to 3 hours, then mash in the avocado and serve. To make the guacamole go further, add 1 medium tomato, seeded and chopped.

CLASSIC DEVILED EGGS

PER SERVING

- ▲ 6 large eggs
- 2 tablespoons finely snipped fresh dill + small dill sprigs
- 2 tablespoons fat-free mayonnaise
- ▲ 1 tablespoon fat-free sour cream
- 1 teaspoon Dijon mustard
- ½ teaspoon white vinegar
- ¼ teaspoon salt
- ¼ teaspoon black pepper

1 Combine eggs with enough cold water to cover by at least 1 inch in medium saucepan; bring to boil. Immediately remove saucepan from heat. Let stand, covered, 15 minutes. Pour off water and cool eggs under cold running water.

2 Peel eggs and cut each lengthwise in half. Transfer yolks to small bowl and mash with fork until smooth. Add all remaining ingredients except dill springs and stir until mixed well.

3 Spoon egg-yolk filling into egg-white halves with spoon or use pastry bag fitted with star tip. Serve or cover loosely with plastic wrap and refrigerate up to 6 hours. Top each egg with dill sprig.

PER SERVING (2 deviled eggs): 85 Cal, 5 g Total Fat, 2 g Sat Fat, 0 g Trans Fat, 213 mg Chol, 225 mg Sod, 2 g Carb, 1 g Sugar, 0 g Fib, 6 g Prot, 29 mg Calc.

★ **FYI** ★ To change up the deviled eggs, add a few tablespoons of minced red bell pepper and season with a bit of curry powder.

CLASSIC DEVILED EGGS

LAYERED REFRIED BEAN DIP

SERVES 16   **20 MIN**

2 PointsPlus© value

PER SERVING

▲ 1 cup fat-free salsa

▲ 1 (16-ounce) can fat-free refried beans

▲ 1 cup lightly packed thinly sliced escarole

▲ 1 large tomato, chopped

▲ 1 small red onion, finely chopped

▲ ⅓ cup fat-free sour cream

½ Haas avocado, pitted, peeled, and thinly sliced

2 tablespoons chopped fresh cilantro

4 ounces baked tortilla chips

1   Stir together ¾ cup of salsa and the beans in small bowl.

2   To assemble, layer ingredients in 1½-quart glass bowl as follows: bean mixture, escarole, tomato, onion, and remaining ¼ cup salsa. Dollop sour cream in center, then top with avocado and sprinkle with cilantro. Serve with tortilla chips.

PER SERVING (¼ cup dip and about 4 chips): 76 Cal, 2 g Total Fat, 1 g Sat Fat, 0 g Trans Fat, 1 mg Chol, 271 mg Sod, 13 g Carb, 2 g Sugar, 3 g Fib, 3 g Prot, 32 mg Calc.

★ **FYI** ★   This dip can be assembled up to 6 hours ahead, but top it with the sour cream, avocado, and cilantro just before serving.

7 PointsPlus® value
PER SERVING

SERVES 6

1 Heat oil in Dutch oven over medium heat. Add chopped onion, red and green bell peppers, and garlic; cook, stirring, until onion is softened, about 5 minutes. Stir in cumin and cook, stirring, until fragrant, about 1 minute. Stir in beans and broth; cook, stirring occasionally, 15 minutes.

2 Transfer 1 cup of bean mixture to blender or food processor and puree. Stir puree back into soup. Stir in chicken and vinegar; cook, stirring occasionally, until heated through, about 4 minutes. If soup seems thick, stir in some water.

3 Ladle soup evenly into 6 bowls. Top each serving with one-sixth of tomatoes, 1 tablespoon of sour cream, 1 tablespoon of red onion, and scant tablespoon of cilantro.

PER SERVING (about 1½ cups). 289 Cal, 6 g Total Fat, 1 g Sat Fat, 0 g Trans Fat, 50 mg Chol, 557 mg Sod, 30 g Carb, 4 g Sugar, 8 g Fib, 28 g Prot, 102 mg Calc.

- 1 tablespoon canola oil
- ▲ 1 onion, chopped
- ▲ ½ red bell pepper, diced
- ▲ ½ green bell pepper, diced
- 3 large garlic cloves, minced
- 2 teaspoons ground cumin
- ▲ 2 (15 ½-ounce) cans black beans, rinsed and drained
- ▲ 3 cups reduced-sodium chicken broth
- ▲ ¾ pound cooked skinless boneless fat-free chicken breasts, shredded
- 2 tablespoons white vinegar
- ▲ 1 cup cherry tomatoes, quartered
- ▲ 6 tablespoons fat-free sour cream
- ▲ 6 tablespoons finely chopped red onion
- 4 tablespoons chopped fresh cilantro

ALL AMERICAN

Little Havana, a neighborhood in Miami, Florida, is home to the many Cuban immigrants who emigrated there in the 1960s. It is named after Havana, the capital of Cuba. This soup is very similar to ones you might enjoy in one of Little Havana's restaurants.

YELLOW SPLIT PEA SOUP

1 Heat oil in Dutch oven over medium heat. Add onion, carrots, celery, and oregano; cook, stirring, until onion is golden, about 8 minutes.

2 Add remaining ingredients and bring to boil over medium-high heat. With slotted spoon, skim off any foam that rises to surface. Reduce heat and simmer, covered, until split peas fall apart, about 1 hour. Remove bay leaf and discard.

3 With slotted spoon, transfer ham hock to cutting board; let cool. Discard skin and bones. Finely chop meat and stir into soup. Cook over medium heat until heated through, about 4 minutes.

PER SERVING (1 cup): 298 Cal, 7 g Total Fat, 1 g Sat Fat, 0 g Trans Fat, 13 mg Chol, 360 mg Sod, 42 g Carb, 3 g Sugar, 19 g Fib, 18 g Prot, 40 mg Calc.

2 tablespoons canola oil

▲ 1 large onion, chopped

▲ 2 carrots, diced

▲ 2 celery stalks, diced

1 teaspoon dried oregano

▲ 1 (1-pound) package dried yellow split peas, picked over, rinsed, and drained

▲ 1 (32-ounce) carton reduced-sodium chicken broth

2 cups water

1 smoked ham hock (about ½-pound)

½ teaspoon salt

½ teaspoon black pepper

1 bay leaf

★ **FYI** ★ Add 2 large potatoes, diced and cooked, to the soup in step 3. This will increase the per-serving *PointsPlus* value by **1**.

AUTUMN SQUASH, APPLE, AND MUSHROOM SOUP

SERVES 6

PER SERVING

- ▲ 2 acorn squash (about ¾ pound each), halved and seeded
- 1 tablespoon olive oil
- ▲ 1 onion, chopped
- ▲ 2 celery stalks, chopped
- ▲ 2 McIntosh apples, peeled, cored, and chopped
- ▲ 8 ounces cremini or white mushrooms, sliced
- ▲ 1 (32-ounce) carton reduced-sodium vegetable broth
- ¼ teaspoon black pepper

1 Preheat oven to 350°F. Line large baking sheet with foil.

2 Place squash, cut side down, on foil. Bake until tender, about 45 minutes. When cool enough to handle, scoop out flesh and discard skin.

3 Heat oil in large saucepan over medium heat. Add onion and celery; cook, stirring, until softened, about 5 minutes. Add apples and mushrooms; cook, stirring, until apples begin to soften, about 5 minutes. Stir in squash, broth, and pepper; cook, stirring occasionally, until apples are very tender and flavors are blended, about 15 minutes.

4 Remove saucepan from heat and let soup cool about 5 minutes. Puree soup, in batches, in blender. Return soup to saucepan and cook until heated through, about 5 minutes.

PER SERVING (about 1 cup): 111 Cal, 3 g Total Fat, 0 g Sat Fat, 0 g Trans Fat, 0 mg Chol, 118 mg Sod, 22 g Carb, 11 g Sugar, 4 g Fib, 2 g Prot, 5 mg Calc.

★ **FYI** ★ You can substitute butternut squash for the acorn squash if you like. Top each serving of soup with a dollop of fat-free sour cream (2 tablespoons of reduced-fat sour cream per serving will increase the *PointsPlus* value by **1**).

PEANUT SOUP

1 Spray large nonstick saucepan with nonstick spray and set over medium heat. Add onion and chili powder; cook, stirring, until onion is softened, about 5 minutes. Stir in peanut butter, flour, and cayenne; cook, stirring, 1 minute.

2 Gradually whisk broth into onion mixture and bring to boil. Reduce heat and simmer, covered, 15 minutes. Stir in milk, salt, and pepper sauce; cook, stirring, until heated through, about 3 minutes longer.

PER SERVING (about ¾ cup): 156 Cal, 7 g Total Fat, 2 g Sat Fat, 0 g Trans Fat, 1 mg Chol, 489 mg Sod, 16 g Carb, 5 g Sugar, 2 g Fib, 9 g Prot, 53 mg Calc.

- 1 small onion, finely chopped
- 2 teaspoons chili powder
- ¼ cup reduced-fat peanut butter
- 2 tablespoons all-purpose flour
- Pinch cayenne
- 2½ cups reduced-sodium chicken broth
- ½ cup fat-free milk
- ½ teaspoon salt
- Few drops hot pepper sauce or to taste

ALL AMERICAN

Peanuts were first cultivated in South America and eventually brought to America by slaves. George Washington Carver (1861–1943) the son of a slave, was a chemist, inventor, and educator who developed products made from peanuts, sweet potatoes, and soybeans. He promoted peanut soup as one of the many ways to enjoy this nutritious legume.

SHE-CRAB SOUP

SERVES 6 ....

PER SERVING

2 teaspoons canola oil

3 shallots, finely chopped

▲ 1 celery stalk, chopped

3 tablespoons all-purpose flour

4 cups low-fat (1%) milk

▲ ½ pound lump crabmeat, picked over

¼ cup dry sherry

½ teaspoon salt

¼ teaspoon black pepper

Pinch cayenne or to taste

Paprika

1 Heat oil in large saucepan over medium heat. Add shallots and celery; cook, stirring, until softened, about 5 minutes. Sprinkle flour over vegetables and cook, stirring, about 2 minutes. Gradually stir in milk; cook 5 minutes.

2 Add crabmeat, sherry, salt, black pepper, and cayenne to soup. Cook until heated through, about 3 minutes. Ladle soup evenly into 6 bowls. Sprinkle with paprika.

PER SERVING (about 1 cup): 140 Cal, 3 g Total Fat, 1 g Sat Fat, 0 g Trans Fat, 23 mg Chol, 428 mg Sod, 16 g Carb, 9 g Sugar, 0 g Fib, 11 g Prot, 219 mg Calc.

ALL AMERICAN

Both Charleston and Savannah claim to be the creators of this delectably rich and creamy soup. Traditionally, the roe of female crabs is what gives this soup it's special flavor—and name.

SHE-CRAB SOUP, WITH TOASTED SESAME
CHEESE STRAWS, PAGE 39

NEW ENGLAND–STYLE WILD SALMON CHOWDER

SERVES 8 ....

PER SERVING

2 slices turkey bacon

1 tablespoon canola oil

▲ 1 onion, chopped

▲ 3 celery stalks, diced

▲ 2 baking potatoes, peeled and cut into ½-inch cubes

2 (8-ounce) bottles clam juice

▲ 1 pound wild salmon or halibut, cut into ¾-inch chunks

▲ 1 cup fresh or thawed frozen corn kernels

▲ 1 pint fat-free half-and-half

½ teaspoon dried oregano

¼ teaspoon black pepper

⅓ cup finely chopped fresh parsley

1   Cook bacon in Dutch oven over medium heat until crisp. With slotted spoon, transfer bacon to paper towel–lined plate to drain. Wipe pot clean.

2   Heat oil in Dutch oven over medium heat. Add onion and celery; cook, stirring, until softened, about 5 minutes. Add potatoes and clam juice; bring to boil. Reduce heat and simmer, covered, until potatoes are tender, about 15 minutes.

3   Add salmon, corn, half-and-half, oregano, and pepper to pot. Simmer, covered, just until fish is opaque in center, about 5 minutes. Ladle soup evenly among 8 soup bowls. Crumble bacon; sprinkle bacon and parsley over chowder.

PER SERVING (generous 1 cup): 213 Cal, 7 g Total Fat, 1 g Sat Fat, 0 g Trans Fat, 41 mg Chol, 307 mg Sod, 19 g Carb, 7 g Sugar, 2 g Fib, 18 g Prot, 118 mg Calc.

★ **FYI** ★   To get 1 cup of fresh corn kernels you will need about 2 medium ears of corn.

3
PointsPlus®
value

PER SERVING

SERVES 6

1 Heat oil in large saucepan over medium heat. Add onion and cook, stirring, until softened, about 5 minutes. Stir in potatoes, clam juice, ½ cup of water, and thyme; bring to simmer. Cook, covered, until potatoes are tender, about 12 minutes.

2 Whisk together remaining ⅓ cup water and the flour in small bowl until smooth. Whisk flour mixture into saucepan until blended well. Cook, stirring, until soup bubbles and thickens, about 2 minutes.

3 Stir remaining ingredients into soup. Reduce heat to low and cook until heated through, about 2 minutes (do not boil).

PER SERVING (about 1 cup): 109 Cal, 2 g Total Fat, 0 g Sat Fat, 0 g Trans Fat, 14 mg Chol, 523 mg Sod, 15 g Carb, 6 g Sugar, 1 g Fib, 9 g Prot, 121 mg Calc.

2 teaspoons olive oil

▲ 1 onion, chopped

▲ ½ pound red potatoes, scrubbed and cut into ½-inch dice

1 (8-ounce) bottle clam juice

½ + ⅓ cup water

2 teaspoons chopped fresh thyme

2 tablespoons all-purpose flour

▲ 2 (6½-ounce) cans chopped clams, drained

▲ 2 cups fat-free milk

2 tablespoons chopped fresh flat-leaf parsley

¼ teaspoon black pepper

⅛ teaspoon liquid hickory smoke

ALL AMERICAN

Chowders have been a staple in New England cooking since the early 1700s, but back then fish—not clams—were used. A soup is considered a chowder when it is rich and thick with chunky ingredients.

LET YOUR BLENDER, PROCESSOR, OR FOOD MILL DO THE WORK

Blenders, along with other kitchen tools, can really cut down on kitchen prep time:

• **Blender** The idea of putting a blade at the bottom of a covered container was developed by Stephen Poplawski in 1922 to facilitate the making of soda fountain treats. In 1935, Fred Osius made some small improvements to the blender and came up with the widely recognized Waring version. By 1954, one million blenders had been sold. Most blenders come with a glass pitcher that holds anywhere from 48 ounces to 60 ounces and has a tight-fitting lid with an easy-pour spout. The lid comes with a clear measured removable pour cup to make adding ingredients easy. The simplest blenders feature high, low, pulse, and off buttons, while other models offer as few as 5 and as many as 12 touch-pad buttons that enable the blender to blend, puree, chop, liquefy, whip, stir, crush ice, and pulse.
BEST USES: soups, drinks and smoothies, sauces, dips, salad dressings, marinades

• **Food Processor** Having a food processor in your kitchen is like having an extra pair of hands: it chops, slices, grates, shreds, purees, and blends in record time. Back in the early 1970s, Carl Sondheimer, an American engineer, saw a machine called the Robot Coupe—the first food processor—at a trade show in Paris and thought it had great potential in the American market. Back home, he founded the Cuisinart company and made improvements to the machine. Sales took off when James Beard, Julia Child, and Craig Claiborne developed recipes based on using the food processor.
BEST USES: slicing or shredding potatoes and other vegetables, vegetable and fruit purees, pie dough, soups, sauces, salad dressings

• **Immersion Blender** Also known as a stick blender or hand blender, this handy portable kitchen tool allows the cook to puree or blend foods right in the pot or bowl they are made in. The cook holds the end of the blender that contains the motor. Extending from it is a long metal rod with a small blade at the end. A two-speed motor is regulated by pressing a toggle button located on the handle. The key to using an immersion blender is to immerse it in the food before turning on the motor to avoid splashing. Some newer models come with a beaker and whisk attachment, which makes it easy to whip up a small batch of cream and to make salad dressings and sauces.
BEST USES: soups, vegetable and fruit purees, sauces

• **Food Mill** Using a food mill is an easy non-electric way to puree foods. In its simplest form, it is made up of two parts: a long-handled bowl with small holes covering the bottom and a hand crank that has a bent metal blade which crushes or purees food as it is forced through the holes. Two or three small feet at the base of the bowl make it easy to set the food mill over a pot or bowl. Other models come with three separate grinding disks to produce fine, medium, and coarse textures. In some models the feet are non-slip and fold in for easy storage, and the handle is soft and non-slip for comfort. Food mills range in price from $12 to over $100, ensuring that there is a model to fit every budget.
BEST USES: soups, vegetable purees, applesauce, mashed potatoes

RED, WHITE, AND BLUE POTATO SALAD

3 PointsPlus® value

PER SERVING

1 Put potatoes in large saucepan and add enough cold water to cover; bring to boil. Reduce heat and simmer, covered, until potatoes are tender, about 12 minutes. Drain.

2 Transfer hot potatoes to serving bowl; sprinkle with 1 tablespoon of vinegar and toss to coat evenly. Add fennel, onion, bell pepper, mint, and egg; gently toss to combine well.

3 To make dressing, whisk together ingredients until smooth, adding 1–2 tablespoons of water to thin dressing if needed. Drizzle dressing over potato mixture; stir gently to combine well. Serve or cover and refrigerate up to 6 hours.

PER SERVING (⅔ cup): 127 Cal, 2 g Total Fat, 1 g Sat Fat, 0 g Trans Fat, 27 mg Chol, 310 mg Sod, 24 g Carb, 3 g Sugar, 2 g Fib, 4 g Prot, 37 mg Calc.

▲ 2 pounds mixed small red, fingerling, and purple potatoes, scrubbed and cut into ¾-inch dice

1 tablespoon cider vinegar

▲ ½ cup chopped fennel or celery

▲ 1 small onion, finely chopped

▲ ½ small red bell pepper, chopped

¼ cup finely chopped fresh mint, parsley, or chives or a combination

▲ 1 hard-cooked large egg, peeled and chopped

DRESSING

⅓ cup reduced-fat mayonnaise

▲ ⅓ cup fat-free sour cream

2 tablespoons cider vinegar

1 tablespoon Dijon mustard

1 teaspoon sugar

½ teaspoon salt

¼ teaspoon black pepper

PASTA SALAD WITH LEMON MAYONNAISE

SERVES 6

PER SERVING

▲ 8 ounces whole wheat penne

▲ ½ pound green beans, cut into 1-inch pieces

DRESSING

¼ cup reduced-fat mayonnaise

8 fresh basil leaves, coarsely chopped

Grated zest and juice of ½ lemon

1 teaspoon whole grain mustard

½ teaspoon salt

▲ 1 red bell pepper, diced

▲ 2 celery stalks including leaves, stalks thinly sliced and leaves torn

¼ cup chopped pitted green olives

1 Cook pasta according to package directions, omitting salt if desired and adding green beans during last 5 minutes of cooking time. Drain and rinse under cold running water. Drain again.

2 To make dressing, whisk together mayonnaise, basil, lemon zest and juice, mustard, and salt in serving bowl. Add pasta, green beans, bell pepper, celery, and olives; toss to coat well. Serve or cover and refrigerate up to 1 day.

PER SERVING (generous 1 cup): 187 Cal, 3 g Total Fat, 0 g Sat Fat, 0 g Trans Fat, 0 mg Chol, 394 mg Sod, 35 g Carb, 4 g Sugar, 6 g Fib, 6 g Prot, 41 mg Calc.

★ **FYI** ★ Add 1 cup of halved grape tomatoes along with the vegetables in step 2.

PASTA SALAD WITH LEMON MAYONNAISE

CUCUMBER-DILL SALAD WITH SOUR CREAM DRESSING

SERVES 4   20 MIN

PER SERVING

- ▲ 2 cucumbers (about 1 pound), peeled and thinly sliced
- ▲ 1 small red onion, thinly sliced

¼ cup reduced-fat sour cream

1 tablespoon red wine vinegar

¼ cup snipped fresh dill

½ teaspoon salt

¼ teaspoon black pepper

Mix together ingredients in serving bowl. Serve at once or refrigerate, covered, up to 1 day.

PER SERVING (¼ of salad): 48 Cal, 2 g Total Fat, 1 g Sat Fat, 0 g Trans Fat, 5 mg Chol, 305 mg Sod, 5 g Carb, 2 g Sugar, 1 g Fib, 2 g Prot, 42 mg Calc.

★ **FYI** ★ There are several types of cucumbers available in supermarkets: *Common American cucumbers* have seeds that can be left in or scraped out. They are available year-round. *Kirby cucumbers* are crunchy and sweet. *Persian (mini) cucumbers, slender and curved,* are ideal for Middle Eastern salads.

MASHED POTATOES WITH ROASTED GARLIC

PER SERVING

1 Preheat oven to 400°F. Cut top third off head of garlic and discard. Wrap garlic in foil and roast until softened, about 45 minutes. Unwrap and let cool.

2 Meanwhile, combine potatoes with enough cold water to cover in large saucepan and bring to boil. Reduce heat and simmer, partially covered, until tender, about 20 minutes. Drain potatoes and return to pot. With potato masher, mash potatoes until smooth.

3 Separate garlic cloves and squeeze pulp into potatoes. Add milk, oil, salt, and pepper; stir until mixed.

½ head of garlic

▲ 1½ pounds Yukon Gold potatoes, peeled and cut into 1-inch chunks

▲ ⅓ cup fat-free milk, warmed

1 tablespoon olive oil

½ teaspoon salt

¼ teaspoon black pepper

PER SERVING (1 cup): 159 Cal, 4 g Total Fat, 1 g Sat Fat, 0 g Trans Fat, 0 mg Chol, 301 mg Sod, 32 g Carb, 5 g Sugar, 4 g Fib, 6 g Prot, 58 mg Calc.

★ **FYI** ★ There are three types of potatoes: high starch, low starch, and all purpose. *Baking potatoes* are high-starch potatoes. They cook up fluffy and dry, making them ideal for mashing and baking. *Red and white potatoes* are low-starch and are excellent in salads and stews. *Yukon Gold potatoes* are all-purpose potatoes that have a medium amount of starch.

CREAMED CORN

SERVES 6 | 20 MIN

2 teaspoons unsalted butter

1½ teaspoons all-purpose flour

▲ 2 cups fresh or thawed frozen corn kernels

▲ ½ small red bell pepper, cut into ¼-inch dice

▲ ½ small green bell pepper, cut into ¼-inch dice

1½ teaspoons cornstarch

½ teaspoon salt

¼ teaspoon black pepper

⅔ cup low-fat (1%) milk

Melt butter in medium saucepan over medium heat. Whisk in flour and cook, whisking constantly, 1 minute. Stir in corn, red and green bell peppers, cornstarch, salt, and pepper; cook, stirring, 4 minutes. Gradually add milk and simmer, stirring, until mixture bubbles and thickens and corn is tender, about 3 minutes longer.

PER SERVING (about ⅔ cup): 75 Cal, 2 g Total Fat, 1 g Sat Fat, 0 g Trans Fat, 5 mg Chol, 214 mg Sod, 13 g Carb, 3 g Sugar, 2 g Fib, 3 g Prot, 35 mg Calc.

ALL AMERICAN

It is interesting to note that an average ear of corn contains 800 kernels lined up in 16 rows, while one pound of corn contains about 1,300 kernels. The Native Americans revered corn, calling it the "Sacred Mother." The early colonists easily took to corn, serving it at the first Plymouth Thanksgiving in place of wheat and barley, grains they enjoyed back home in England.

FRESH CORN AND CHIVE SPOON BREAD

SERVES 6

1 Combine corn and ¼ cup of milk in blender or food processor and puree. Pour remaining 1¾ cups milk into large saucepan and bring to boil. Reduce heat to medium and gradually whisk in cornmeal. Cook, stirring occasionally, until thickened, about 5 minutes. Stir in pureed corn, chives, butter, salt, and pepper, stirring until butter is melted. Scrape mixture into large bowl and let cool 10 minutes.

2 Meanwhile, preheat oven to 375°F Spray shallow 2 quart baking dish, casserole dish, or cast-iron skillet with nonstick spray and place in oven to preheat.

3 With electric mixer on medium speed, beat egg whites in medium bowl until stiff peaks form when beaters are lifted. With rubber spatula, stir egg yolks and baking powder into cornmeal mixture; fold in beaten egg whites just until whites are no longer visible.

4 Wearing oven mitts, remove baking dish from oven. Pour cornmeal mixture into baking dish. Bake until spoon bread is puffed and browned, 35–40 minutes. Serve immediately.

- 1 cup fresh or thawed frozen corn kernels
- 2 cups fat-free milk
- ½ cup stone-ground cornmeal
- ¼ cup snipped fresh chives
- 2 tablespoons unsalted butter, cut into pieces
- ¼ teaspoon salt
- ¼ teaspoon black pepper
- 3 large eggs, separated and at room temperature
- 1½ teaspoons baking powder

PER SERVING (⅙ of spoon bread): 150 Cal, 7 g Total Fat, 3 g Sat Fat, 0 g Trans Fat, 119 mg Chol, 310 mg Sod, 18 g Carb, 5 g Sugar, 2 g Fib, 7 g Prot, 144 mg Calc.

★ **FYI** ★ Beating egg whites when they are at room temperature ensures that they will whip up as high as possible. Keep in mind, however, that it is easiest to separate eggs while cold.

CABBAGE IN CARAWAY-SOUR CREAM SAUCE

SERVES 4

PER SERVING

2 teaspoons canola oil

▲ 1 head Savoy cabbage, thinly sliced

½ teaspoon salt

1 tablespoon caraway seeds

1½ teaspoons cider vinegar

1 teaspoon sugar

▲ ½ cup fat-free sour cream

2 tablespoons chopped fresh parsley

1 Heat oil in large nonstick skillet over medium heat. Add cabbage and salt; cook, covered, stirring occasionally, until cabbage is wilted, about 10 minutes.

2 Add caraway seeds, vinegar, and sugar to cabbage, stirring until mixed well. Remove skillet from heat; add sour cream and stir until coated evenly. Serve sprinkled with parsley.

PER SERVING (about 1 cup): 73 Cal, 3 g Total Fat, 0 g Sat Fat, 0 g Trans Fat, 3 mg Chol, 357 mg Sod, 11 g Carb, 2 g Sugar, 3 g Fib, 3 g Prot, 78 mg Calc.

★ **FYI** ★ Savoy cabbage is a mellow-flavored cabbage that was first cultivated in Italy. It is primarily available in the fall. Look for heads with darker green leaves that show no signs of browning.

CREAMY SPINACH WITH PARMESAN

20 MIN   SERVES 4

1 Put spinach in steamer basket; set in large pot over 1 inch of boiling water (the leaves will be tightly packed but will reduce in volume as they wilt). Cover tightly and steam until bright green, about 2 minutes. Drain in colander; when spinach is cool enough to handle, squeeze out excess moisture.

2 Whisk together milk, flour, and pepper together in medium saucepan until blended. Bring to simmer over medium heat, whisking constantly; cook until slightly thickened, about 2 minutes. Whisk in Parmesan. Add spinach and cook, stirring constantly, just until heated through, about 2 minutes.

▲ 2 (9-ounce) bags baby spinach

⅔ cup low-fat (1%) milk

1 tablespoon all-purpose flour

⅛ teasoon black pepper

¼ cup grated Parmesan

PER SERVING (½ cup): 83 Cal, 3 g Total Fat, 2 g Sat Fat, 0 g Trans Fat, 7 mg Chol, 232 mg Sod, 9 g Carb, 3 g Sugar, 3 g Fib, 8 g Prot, 261 mg Calc.

LEMON-AND-HERB–STUFFED
PORK CHOPS, PAGE 129

SAVORY

★ MAIN DISHES ★

Succulent Pot Roast with Root Vegetables, 123

Beef Stew with Fire-Roasted Tomatoes and Bacon, 124

Blue Plate Meat Loaf with Mushroom Gravy, 125

Mushroom and Golden Onion Bison Burgers, 126

Weekend Spaghetti and Meatballs, 128

Lemon-and-Herb–Stuffed Pork Chops, 129

Country Ham and Red-Eye Gravy, 131

Braised Lamb with Smoky Tomatoes, Orange, and Fennel, 132

Crisp Roast Chicken with Herbed Potatoes and Shallots, 134

Hearty Chicken with Parsley Dumplings, 135

Chicken Pizzaiola with Torn Basil and Capers, 137

Turkey, Spinach, and Mushroom Lasagna, 138

Thyme-Crusted Turkey Pot Pie, 141

Cape Cod Clambake, 142

Mussels in Spicy Tomato Broth, 144

★ SOUPS ★

Rich Chicken and Matzo Ball Soup, 145

Fisherman's Wharf Chowder, 147

Manhattan Clam Chowder with Bacon and Potatoes, 148

★ SIDES ★

Butter-and-Sugar-Glazed Carrots and Onions, 149

Hoppin' John, 150

Bacon, Rice, and Bell Pepper Perloo, 151

Farmers' Market Tomato and Goat Cheese Salad, 152

Whole Wheat–Blueberry Griddle Cakes, 154

Oyster-Bacon Dressing, 155

★ BREADS ★

Boston Brown Bread, 156

Sweet Potato Biscuits, 157

SUCCULENT POT ROAST
WITH ROOT VEGETABLES

PER SERVING

1 Combine flour, ½ teaspoon of salt, and ½ teaspoon of pepper in large zip-close plastic bag; add roast. Squeeze out air and seal bag; turn to coat meat.

2 Heat oil in large Dutch oven over medium-high heat. Add roast and cook until browned on all sides, about 8 minutes. Transfer roast to plate. Add onion to pot and cook, stirring, until softened, about 5 minutes. Reduce heat to medium. Add wine and cook, scraping up browned bits from bottom of pot. Stir in broth, mustard, and bay leaves.

3 Return roast to pot and bring to boil. Reduce heat and simmer, covered, 1 hour 30 minutes. Add potatoes, carrots, and parsnips to pot; sprinkle with remaining ½ teaspoon salt and ¼ teaspoon pepper. Cook, covered, until meat is fork-tender and vegetables are tender, about 45 minutes.

4 Transfer roast to cutting board. With slotted spoon, transfer vegetables to serving bowl. Remove bay leaves and discard. Skim off any fat from pan liquid; transfer pan juices to gravy boat. Cut meat across grain into 16 slices.

PER SERVING (2 slices meat, ⅛ of vegetables, and about ⅓ cup pan juices,): 478 Cal, 6 g Total Fat, 1 g Sat Fat, 0 g Trans Fat, 38 mg Chol, 469 mg Sod, 75 g Carb, 9 g Sugar, 10 g Fib, 28 g Prot, 81 mg Calc.

¼ cup all-purpose flour

1 teaspoon salt

¾ teaspoon black pepper

▲ 1 (1½-pound) beef eye-round roast, trimmed

1 tablespoon canola oil

▲ 1 large onion, chopped

1 cup dry white wine

▲ 1 (14½-ounce) can reduced-sodium beef broth

2 tablespoons Dijon mustard

2 bay leaves

▲ 16 small Yukon Gold potatoes, scrubbed and halved

▲ 4 large carrots, cut on diagonal into 1½-inch lengths

▲ 4 parsnips, halved lengthwise and cut on diagonal into 1½-inch lengths

★ **FYI** ★ To end your meal on a light note, toss together a mix of berries, sliced kiwifruit, and diced banana.

BEEF STEW WITH FIRE-ROASTED TOMATOES AND BACON

SERVES 4

PER SERVING

2 tablespoons all-purpose flour

¼ teaspoon salt

½ teaspoon black pepper

▲ 1 (1-pound) beef top round steak, trimmed and cut into 1-inch chunks

1 tablespoon canola oil

▲ 1 onion, sliced

3 garlic cloves, minced

1 cup water

▲ 1 (14 ½-ounce) can fired-roasted diced tomatoes

▲ 1 pound all-purpose potatoes, peeled and cut into 1-inch chunks

▲ 4 carrots, cut into 1½-inch lengths

3 fresh thyme sprigs or 1 teaspoon dried thyme

2 slices turkey bacon, crisp cooked and crumbled

1 Combine flour, salt, and ¼ teaspoon of pepper in large zip-close plastic bag; add beef. Squeeze out air and seal bag; shake bag to coat meat.

2 Heat oil in nonstick Dutch oven over medium-high heat. Add beef, in batches, and cook until browned on all sides, about 4 minutes per batch, transferring beef to medium bowl as it is browned. Add onion and garlic to pot; cook, stirring, until onion is softened, about 5 minutes. Add water and cook, scraping up browned bits from bottom of pot.

3 Return beef to pot along with tomatoes; bring to boil. Reduce heat and simmer, covered, 45 minutes. Add potatoes, carrots, thyme, and remaining ¼ teaspoon pepper; cook, covered until beef is fork-tender and vegetables are tender, about 45 minutes longer. Remove thyme sprigs. Serve sprinkled with bacon.

PER SERVING (about 1½ cups): 373 Cal, 11 g Total Fat, 3 g Sat Fat, 0 g Trans Fat, 63 mg Chol, 619 mg Sod, 38 g Carb, 11 g Sugar, 6 g Fib, 34 g Prot, 80 mg Calc.

★ **FYI** ★ To enhance the smoky flavor in this stew, add a few drops of hickory liquid smoke along with the vegetables in step 3.

BLUE PLATE MEAT LOAF WITH MUSHROOM GRAVY

7 PointsPlus® value

PER SERVING

1 Preheat oven to 350°F. Spray jelly-roll pan with nonstick spray.

2 Meanwhile, heat oil in medium nonstick skillet over medium-high heat. Add mushrooms, onion, and garlic; cook, stirring occasionally, until mushrooms release their liquid and it is evaporated, about 10 minutes. Remove skillet from heat and let cool slightly.

3 Transfer half of mushroom mixture to large bowl. Add beef, bread crumbs, ketchup, egg, mustard, and salt to bowl; stir until blended but not overmixed.

4 Transfer meat loaf mixture to prepared baking pan and shape into 4 x 8-inch loaf. Bake until instant-read thermometer inserted into center of loaf registers 160°F for well done, about 1 hour 10 minutes. Let stand 10 minutes.

5 Meanwhile, whisk together broth, flour, and Worcestershire sauce in cup until smooth. Add to remaining mushroom mixture in skillet; bring to boil. Reduce heat and simmer, stirring occasionally, until sauce bubbles and thickens, about 3 minutes. Cut meat loaf into 12 slices. Serve with sauce.

2 teaspoons olive oil

¾ pound shiitake mushrooms, stems removed and caps sliced

1 large onion, finely chopped

2 garlic cloves, minced

1½ pounds ground lean beef (7% fat or less)

½ cup plain dried whole wheat bread crumbs

¼ cup ketchup

1 large egg, lightly beaten

1 tablespoon Dijon mustard

½ teaspoon salt

1¼ cups reduced-sodium chicken broth

2 teaspoons all-purpose flour

1 teaspoon Worcestershire sauce

PER SERVING (2 slices meat loaf and ¼ cup sauce): 280 Cal, 9 g Total Fat, 3 g Sat Fat, 0 g Trans Fat, 104 mg Chol, 582 mg Sod, 21 g Carb, 7 g Sugar, 2 g Fib, 27 g Prot, 49 mg Calc.

★ **FYI** ★ To turn this meat loaf into a meal, serve it with steamed green beans or broccoli and a bowl of mashed cooked small Yukon Gold potatoes (3 ounces of cooked and mashed potatoes per serving will increase the ***PointsPlus*** value by *2*).

MUSHROOM AND GOLDEN ONION BISON BURGERS

SERVES 4

PER SERVING

▲ 1 pound ground bison or ground lean beef (5% fat or less)

1 tablespoon Worcestershire sauce

½ teaspoon black pepper

1 tablespoon olive oil

▲ 1 large sweet onion, such as Vidalia, sliced

¼ teaspoon salt

▲ ½ pound mushrooms, such as white, cremini, or oyster, sliced

4 whole wheat English muffins, split and toasted

▲ 4 lettuce leaves

▲ 4 thick tomato slices

1 Mix together bison, Worcestershire sauce, and ¼ teaspoon of pepper in large bowl just until well combined. With damp hands, shape mixture into 4 (½-inch-thick) patties.

2 Heat oil in large nonstick skillet over medium-high heat. Add onion and salt; cook, stirring, until golden, about 8 minutes. Transfer to small bowl and keep warm. Add mushrooms and remaining ¼ teaspoon pepper to skillet; cook, stirring, until mushrooms release their liquid and it is evaporated, about 5 minutes. Transfer to another small bowl and keep warm. Wipe skillet clean.

3 Spray skillet with nonstick spray and set over medium-high heat. Place patties in skillet and cook until instant-read thermometer inserted into side of burger registers 160°F for well done, about 4 minutes per side.

4 Place bottoms of English muffins on each of 4 plates. Top each with 1 lettuce leaf, 1 tomato slice, 1 burger, one-fourth of onion, and one-fourth of mushrooms. Cover with tops of English muffins.

PER SERVING (1 garnished burger): 324 Cal, 8 g Total Fat, 2 g Sat Fat, 0 g Trans Fat, 81 mg Chol, 567 mg Sod, 33 g Carb, 8 g Sugar, 5 g Fib, 32 g Prot, 201 mg Calc.

★ **FYI** ★   Bison, also known as buffalo, is very lean and as flavorful as beef. Ground bison can be found in large supermarkets in 1-pound packages.

MUSHROOM AND GOLDEN ONION BISON BURGERS
AND STEAKHOUSE "FRIES", PAGE 32

WEEKEND SPAGHETTI AND MEATBALLS

SERVES 8

PER SERVING

TOMATO SAUCE

1 tablespoon olive oil

▲ 1 onion, chopped

2 large garlic cloves, minced

▲ 1 (28-ounce) can crushed tomatoes

8 large fresh basil leaves, torn

1 teaspoon dried oregano

½ teaspoon salt

¼ teaspoon black pepper

MEATBALLS

1 tablespoon olive oil

▲ ½ pound white mushrooms, finely chopped

▲ 1 onion, chopped

▲ ¾ pound ground lean beef (7% fat or less)

⅓ cup grated Parmesan cheese

2 tablespoons plain dried whole wheat bread crumbs

½ teaspoon salt

¼ teaspoon black pepper

▲ 1 pound whole wheat spaghetti

1 Preheat oven to 350°F. Spray jelly-roll pan with nonstick spray.

2 To make sauce, heat oil in large Dutch oven over medium heat. Add onion and garlic; cook, stirring, until onion is softened, about 5 minutes. Stir in remaining sauce ingredients; cook, stirring occasionally, until sauce is slightly thickened, about 20 minutes.

3 Meanwhile, to make meatballs, heat oil in large nonstick skillet over medium-high heat. Add mushrooms and onion; cook until onion is lightly browned and mushrooms are softened, about 6 minutes. Transfer to large bowl and let cool slightly.

4 Add beef, Parmesan, bread crumbs, salt, and pepper to onion mixture. With damp hands, form mixture into 16 meatballs and place in prepared baking pan. Bake until browned and cooked through, about 20 minutes.

5 Meanwhile, cook spaghetti according to package directions, omitting salt if desired. Drain and keep warm. Add meatballs to tomato sauce; cook, stirring occasionally, until heated through, about 10 minutes. Serve over spaghetti.

PER SERVING (1 cup spaghetti, 2 meatballs, and about ½ cup sauce): 351 Cal, 8 g Total Fat, 2 g Sat Fat, 0 g Trans Fat, 29 mg Chol, 596 mg Sod, 54 g Carb, 4 g Sugar, 10 g Fib, 21 g Prot, 112 mg Calc.

ALL AMERICAN

From 1892 to 1943, New York's Ellis Island was teaming with immigrants who came to America in search of a better life. Among the many recipes Italians brought with them was spaghetti and meatballs, which has been embraced all across America and become a classic.

LEMON-AND-HERB-STUFFED PORK CHOPS

PER SERVING

1 Preheat oven to 400°F.

2 To make stuffing, mix together all ingredients except pork chops in medium bowl.

3 Make pocket in each pork chop by inserting small sharp knife into side of chop and cutting back and forth until large, deep pocket is formed. Fill each pocket with about 2 tablespoons of filling.

4 Spray large nonstick ovenproof skillet with nonstick spray and set over medium heat. Add pork chops and cook until golden brown, about 2 minutes per side. Cover skillet and transfer to oven. Roast until pork is almost cooked through, about 5 minutes. Uncover and roast until stuffing is golden and slightly crisp, about 6 minutes longer.

PER SERVING (1 stuffed pork chop): 174 Cal, 6 g Total Fat, 2 g Sat Fat, 0 g Trans Fat, 66 mg Chol, 412 mg Sod, 5 g Carb, 1 g Sugar, 1 g Fib, 23 g Prot, 46 mg Calc.

- 1 small celery stalk, finely chopped
- ½ small onion, finely chopped
- 1 large egg white, lightly beaten

3 tablespoons plain dried whole wheat bread crumbs

1 tablespoon chopped fresh parsley

Grated zest of ½ lemon

½ teaspoon dried thyme

½ teaspoon dried rosemary

½ teaspoon salt

½ teaspoon black pepper

- 4 (¼-pound) boneless pork loin chops, trimmed

★ **FYI** ★ To turn these chops into a complete meal, serve them with steamed red, white, or rainbow Swiss chard and a little unsweetened applesauce.

COUNTRY HAM AND RED-EYE
GRAVY AND SWEET POTATO
BISCUITS, PAGE 157

COUNTRY HAM AND RED-EYE GRAVY

1 Heat oil in large nonstick skillet over medium heat. Add ham and cook until lightly browned, about 4 minutes per side. Transfer to plate and keep warm.

2 To make gravy, whisk together coffee and cornstarch in small bowl until smooth. Pour into skillet and bring to boil. Cook, whisking, until gravy is slightly thickened, about 2 minutes. Serve with ham.

2 teaspoons canola oil

▲ 1 (10-ounce) slice lean hickory-smoked ham, cut into 4 equal pieces

1 cup strong brewed coffee

¾ teaspoon cornstarch

PER SERVING (1 piece ham and ¼ cup gravy) Per serving: 110 Cal, 5 g Total Fat, 1 g Sat Fat, 0 g Trans Fat, 32 mg Chol, 901 mg Sod, 0 g Carb, 0 g Sugar, 0 g Fib, 14 g Prot, 4 mg Calc.

ALL AMERICAN

Ham and red-eye gravy—especially when served with country biscuits or creamy grits—is a favorite Southern breakfast. The gravy got its name from the appearance of a "red eye" that forms in the middle of the gravy as it cooks. Serve this with fried or poached eggs to make it a satisfying main dish. One fried or poached large egg per serving will increase the **PointsPlus** value by **2.**

BRAISED LAMB WITH SMOKY TOMATOES, ORANGE, AND FENNEL

SERVES 10

8
PointsPlus®
value

PER SERVING

1 (2 ¾-pound) boneless leg of lamb, trimmed and tied

1½ teaspoons dried rosemary, crumbled

1 teaspoon salt

½ teaspoon black pepper

▲ 1 onion, chopped

▲ ½ small fennel bulb, chopped

▲ 1 carrot, cut into ¾-inch chunks

▲ ½ pound cremini mushrooms, sliced

▲ 1 tablespoon tomato paste

▲ 1 (14½-ounce) can fire-roasted diced tomatoes, drained

▲ 1 cup reduced-sodium chicken broth

2 strips orange zest, removed with vegetable peeler

3 tablespoons water

1 tablespoon cornstarch

1 Preheat oven to 350°F. Spray large Dutch oven with nonstick spray and set over medium-high heat.

2 Sprinkle lamb with ½ teaspoon of rosemary, ½ teaspoon of salt, and ¼ teaspoon of pepper. Add to Dutch oven and cook until browned on all sides, about 8 minutes; transfer to plate.

3 Spray Dutch oven with nonstick spray. Add onion, fennel, and carrot; cook, stirring, until onion is softened, about 5 minutes. Add mushrooms and cook, stirring occasionally, until softened, about 3 minutes. Stir in tomato paste. Add tomatoes, broth, orange zest, and remaining 1 teaspoon rosemary, ½ teaspoon salt, and ¼ teaspoon pepper; bring to simmer.

4 Return lamb to pot; cover pot and put in oven. Braise until instant-read thermometer inserted into center of roast registers 145°F for medium, about 50 minutes. Transfer lamb to cutting board; let stand 10 minutes.

5 Meanwhile, whisk together water and cornstarch in cup until smooth. Add cornstarch mixture to pot and simmer until pan liquid bubbles and is slightly thickened, about 2 minutes.

6 Cut lamb into 10 slices and arrange on platter. Spoon some sauce with vegetables over lamb. Serve remaining sauce separately.

PER SERVING (1 slice lamb and about ½ cup vegetables with sauce): 286 Cal, 10 g Total Fat, 7 g Sat Fat, 0 g Trans Fat, 164 mg Chol, 574 mg Sod, 9 g Carb, 4 g Sugar, 2 g Fib, 45 g Prot, 53 mg Calc.

★ **FYI** ★ To round out the meal, serve the lamb with a bowl of whole wheat couscous, quinoa, or brown rice (⅔ cup of cooked whole wheat couscous, quinoa, or brown rice per serving will increase the **PointsPlus** value by **3**).

BRAISED LAMB WITH
SMOKY TOMATOES, ORANGE, AND FENNEL

CRISP ROAST CHICKEN WITH HERBED POTATOES AND SHALLOTS

SERVES 6 ....

PER SERVING

1 (3 ½-pound) chicken, giblets removed

1 teaspoon salt

¾ teaspoon black pepper

▲ 3 baking potatoes, scrubbed and each cut into 8 wedges

12 small shallots, peeled

6 large garlic cloves, peeled

2 tablespoons chopped fresh rosemary or thyme

1 tablespoon olive oil

1 Preheat oven to 400°F. Spray medium roasting pan with nonstick spray.

2 With kitchen scissors, cut down along each side of backbone of chicken and discard or save for stock. Place chicken, opened flat, on sheet of wax paper and press down on breastbone to slightly flatten. Sprinkle chicken on both sides with ½ teaspoon of salt and ½ teaspoon of pepper. Place, skin side up, in prepared roasting pan; spray chicken with nonstick spray.

3 Roast chicken until instant-read thermometer inserted in thigh (not touching bone) registers 165°F, about 1 hour, shaking pan once or twice to ensure chicken doesn't stick.

4 Meanwhile, spray medium baking dish with nonstick spray. Combine potatoes, shallots, garlic, rosemary, and remaining ½ teaspoon salt and ¼ teaspoon pepper in baking dish; drizzle with oil and toss until coated evenly. Spread potatoes to form even layer. After chicken has roasted 15 minutes, put baking dish in oven and roast potatoes until crisp and tender, about 45 minutes. Transfer to serving bowl.

5 Transfer chicken to cutting board and let stand 10 minutes. Carve and arrange on platter. Skim off fat from pan juices; pour juices over chicken. Serve vegetables alongside. Remove chicken skin before eating.

PER SERVING (⅙ of chicken, about 2 tablespoons pan juices, and ⅙ of vegetables): 326 Cal, 7 g Total Fat, 2 g Sat Fat, 0 g Trans Fat, 105 mg Chol, 487 mg Sod, 25 g Carb, 3 g Sugar, 2 g Fib, 42 g Prot, 62 mg Calc.

★ **FYI** ★ Butterflying a chicken—removing the backbone, pressing down on the breastbone to flatten it, and opening up the chicken so it lies flat—ensures that it cooks evenly and stays juicy. Another bonus is that a butterflied chicken takes less time to roast.

HEARTY CHICKEN WITH PARSLEY DUMPLINGS

11
PointsPlus®
value

PER SERVING

1 Heat oil in nonstick Dutch oven over medium heat. Add onion and garlic; cook, stirring, until onion is softened, about 5 minutes. Stir in celery, carrots, broth, thyme, and pepper. Add chicken and bring to boil, skimming off any foam that rises to surface. Reduce heat and simmer until chicken is cooked through, about 30 minutes. Transfer chicken to plate and let cool. Separate meat from bones; discard bones.

2 To make dumplings, whisk together egg and milk in medium bowl until frothy. Whisk in 1 cup of flour, the baking powder, and salt. Add remaining 1 cup flour and the parsley, stirring until it forms thick batter.

3 Return broth to simmer over medium-high heat. Reduce heat to medium. Drop batter by about ⅓ cupfuls into broth, making total of 6 dumplings and cook 7 minutes; carefully turn dumplings over. Cook, covered, until dumplings are light and fluffy, about 7 minutes longer.

4 Return chicken to pot and cook until heated through, about 3 minutes longer.

5 Divide chicken, dumplings, sauce, and vegetables evenly among 6 large shallow bowls.

PER SERVING (1 chicken breast, 1 dumpling, and ⅙ of vegetables with sauce): 448 Cal, 9 g Total Fat, 2 g Sat Fat, 0 g Trans Fat, 138 mg Chol, 544 mg Sod, 43 g Carb, 5 g Sugar, 3 g Fib, 47 g Prot, 110 mg Calc.

1 tablespoon canola oil

▲ 1 large onion, coarsely chopped

4 garlic cloves, minced

▲ 3 celery stalks, cut into 1½-inch lengths

▲ 4 carrots, cut into 1½-inch lengths

▲ 1 (32-ounce) carton reduced-sodium chicken broth

2 fresh thyme sprigs

¼ teaspoon black pepper

▲ 6 (½-pound) bone-in chicken breasts, skinned

DUMPLINGS

▲ 1 large egg

▲ ⅓ cup fat-free milk

2 cups all-purpose flour

1½ teaspoons baking powder

½ teaspoon salt

1 tablespoon finely chopped fresh parsley

CHICKEN PIZZAIOLA WITH TORN BASIL AND CAPERS

CHICKEN PIZZAIOLA WITH TORN BASIL AND CAPERS

6 PointsPlus® value

PER SERVING

1 Place chicken between 2 pieces of plastic wrap. With meat pounder or rolling pin, pound to even thickness

2 Sprinkle chicken with oregano, salt, and black pepper. Spray large nonstick skillet with nonstick spray and set over medium-high heat. Add chicken and cook until golden brown, about 1½ minutes per side. Transfer to plate.

3 Add oil to skillet and reduce heat to medium. Add onion and bell pepper; cook, stirring frequently, until onion is lightly golden, about 7 minutes. Add garlic and cook, stirring frequently, until fragrant, about 1 minute. Return chicken to skillet along with marinara sauce, broth, capers, and pepper flakes. Simmer until chicken is cooked through, about 5 minutes longer. Serve sprinkled with Parmesan and basil.

PER SERVING (1 chicken breast and ⅓ cup vegetables with sauce): 257 Cal, 8 g Total Fat, 2 g Sat Fat, 0 g Trans Fat, 83 mg Chol, 586 mg Sod, 12 g Carb, 7 g Sugar, 2 g Fib, 33 g Prot, 113 mg Calc.

- 4 (5-ounce) skinless boneless chicken breasts
- ¾ teaspoon dried oregano
- ½ teaspoon salt
- ¼ teaspoon black pepper
- 2 teaspoons olive oil
- 1 onion, thinly sliced
- 1 red bell pepper, thinly sliced
- 2 large garlic cloves, minced
- 1½ cups no-salt-added marinara sauce
- ½ cup reduced-sodium chicken broth
- 1 tablespoon nonpareil (tiny) capers, drained
- ¼ teaspoon red pepper flakes
- ¼ cup grated Parmesan cheese
- 8 fresh basil leaves, torn

★ **FYI** ★ This Italian-American favorite is often served with spaghetti and a side of steamed green vegetables (1 cup of cooked whole wheat spaghetti per serving will increase the *PointsPlus* value by **4**).

SAVORY   **137**

TURKEY, SPINACH, AND MUSHROOM LASAGNA

SERVES 8

9 PointsPlus® value

PER SERVING

- 1 pound ground skinless turkey breast
- 2 teaspoons olive oil
- 1 small onion, chopped
- 1 (10-ounce) package cremini mushrooms sliced
- 2 large garlic cloves, minced
- 1 (10-ounce) bag spinach, trimmed
- ½ teaspoon salt
- ¼ teaspoon black pepper
- 4 cups no-salt-added marinara sauce
- 1 (8-ounce) box no-boil lasagna noodles (12 noodles)
- 1 (15-ounce) container fat-free ricotta cheese
- 1½ cups shredded part-skim mozzarella cheese
- 8 fresh basil leaves

1   Preheat oven to 375°F. Spray 9 x 13-inch baking dish with nonstick spray.

2   Spray large nonstick skillet with nonstick spray and set over medium-high heat. Add turkey and cook, stirring frequently, until no longer pink, about 5 minutes. Transfer to large bowl. Wipe skillet clean.

3   Add oil to skillet and reduce heat to medium. Add onion and cook, stirring, until softened, about 5 minutes. Add mushrooms and garlic; cook, stirring, until mushrooms are softened, about 5 minutes. Add spinach, salt, and pepper; cook, stirring, until spinach is wilted, about 3 minutes longer. Add mushroom mixture to turkey, stirring to combine.

4   To assemble, spread 1 cup of marinara sauce over bottom of prepared baking dish. Cover with 4 lasagna noodles, overlapping them, if needed. Cover with half of turkey mixture, dot with half of ricotta, and top with 1 cup of marinara sauce. Add another layer of 4 noodles; cover with remaining turkey mixture, remaining ricotta, 1 cup of marinara sauce, and remaining 4 noodles. Spread remaining 1 cup of marinara sauce on top and sprinkle with mozzarella.

5   Spray sheet of foil with nonstick spray; cover dish with foil, sprayed side down, and bake 30 minutes. Remove foil and bake until mozzarella is slightly browned and noodles are very tender, about 20 minutes longer. Let cool 15 minutes before cutting into 8 equal portions. Serve sprinkled with basil.

PER SERVING (⅛ of lasagna): 346 Cal, 7 g Total Fat, 2 g Sat Fat, 0 g Trans Fat, 41 mg Chol, 461 mg Sod, 39 g Carb, 9 g Sugar, 4 g Fib, 32 g Prot, 348 mg Calc.

TURKEY, SPINACH, AND MUSHROOM LASAGNA

ADD FLAVOR WITH FRESH MUSHROOMS

Mushrooms are a type of fungus even though we treat them like a vegetable. They are very versatile, as they can be broiled, grilled, steamed, sautéed, simmered, and eaten raw. There are two basic categories of mushrooms: wild and cultivated. True wild mushrooms are foraged in forests, available only seasonally, and very expensive, while cultivated mushrooms are available year-round and more reasonably priced.

TO CHOOSE: Always pick fresh-looking mushrooms without wrinkles or soft spots.

TO STORE: Wrap the mushrooms in a paper towel and place in an open plastic bag in the crisper drawer of the refrigerator.

TO CLEAN: Either wipe off any dirt with a damp paper towel or lightly wash them under cool running water and pat dry.

NAME	DESCRIPTION	BEST USES
Chanterelles	are delicate, funnel-shaped mushrooms that are yellow to deep golden. Their gills run lengthwise on the outside and taper into a short stem. Chanterelles have been prized in fine French cooking for hundreds of years. Their aroma and flavor is hard to describe. These special mushrooms command a high price so are best saved for special occasions.	sautéed with garlic and parsley, added to pasta or risotto, in sauces
Cremini	are interchangeable with white mushrooms. They have brown caps and a rich, earthy flavor when cooked.	stews, soups, with pasta or risotto, frittatas, omelettes
Enokis	are Japanese mushrooms that grow in small, delicate clumps. They have long creamy white stems, tiny caps, and a mild flavor. They are eaten raw.	Asian-style soups and salads
Lobster	mushrooms are technically not mushrooms at all but a fungus that takes over and encases certain mushrooms. Their deep orange lobsterlike color, craggy shape, and oceanlike aroma and flavor make them popular with seafood.	sautéed, seafood dishes
Portobello	are actually mature creminis. These giant mushrooms have caps that can grow up to six inches in diameter. Their stems are not edible so they are often sold without them. Portobellos have a meaty texture and deep mushroom flavor.	grilled whole or sliced, soups, stews
Shiitake	mushrooms originated in Japan. Their color ranges from medium to deep brown. Their caps are softer than other mushrooms and their stems woody and inedible.	stir-fries, soups, stews
White	are the go-to mushrooms in many recipes, as they have a deep mushroom flavor when cooked and are reasonably priced. They are creamy white and range in size from small to jumbo (great for stuffing). Their delicate flavor when raw makes them a great addition to salads.	sautéed, soups, stews, omelettes, frittatas, pasta sauces, lasagna

THYME-CRUSTED TURKEY POT PIE

11
PointsPlus®
value

PER SERVING

1 To make dough, whisk together flour and salt in medium bowl; stir in thyme. With pastry blender or 2 knives used scissor-fashion, cut shortening into flour mixture until mixture resembles coarse crumbs. With fork, stir in ice water, 1 tablespoon at a time, until dough forms. Shape dough into disk; wrap in plastic wrap and refrigerate at least 30 minutes or up to 1 day.

2 Preheat oven to 400°F.

3 To make filling, bring large saucepan of water to boil. Add potatoes, celery, and carrots; return to boil and cook 3 minutes. Add onions and peas; cook 1 minute longer; drain. Add broth, turkey, and Worcestershire sauce. Bring to a boil and cook 1 minute.

4 Whisk together milk and flour in small bowl until smooth. Stir into turkey mixture and cook until sauce bubbles and thickens, about 1 minute. Remove saucepan from heat. Stir in mustard and salt. Pour into 9-inch deep-dish pie plate or casserole dish.

5 Lightly flour work surface. With floured rolling pin, roll out dough to 12-inch round. Carefully place dough over turkey filling. Tuck edge of dough in against side of dish. With small knife, cut several 1-inch slits to allow steam to escape. Bake until crust is golden and filling is bubbling, about 30 minutes.

PER SERVING (⅙ of pie): 421 Cal, 12 g Total Fat, 3 g Sat Fat, 0 g Trans Fat, 48 mg Chol, 521 mg Sod, 52 g Carb, 9 g Sugar, 5 g Fib, 28 g Prot, 112 mg Calc.

DOUGH

1 cup + 2 tablespoons all-purpose flour

¼ teaspoon salt

1 tablespoon chopped fresh thyme

⅓ cup vegetable shortening, chilled

2–3 tablespoons ice water

FILLING

▲ 3 Yukon Gold potatoes, scrubbed and diced

▲ 2 celery stalks, diced

▲ 2 carrots, diced

▲ 1½ cups frozen pearl onions, thawed

▲ 1½ cups frozen peas, thawed

▲ 2 cups reduced-sodium chicken broth

▲ ¾ pound cooked skinless boneless fat-free turkey breast, cubed

1 tablespoon Worcestershire sauce

▲ 1 cup fat-free milk

2 tablespoons all-purpose flour

1 tablespoon Dijon mustard

½ teaspoon salt

★ **FYI** ★ There are two ways to transfer pie dough to a pie plate: fold the dough in quarters, then place it on top of the filling and unfold it, or roll the dough onto a rolling pin and unroll it over the filling.

CAPE COD CLAMBAKE

▲ 4 red potatoes, scrubbed and each cut into 8 wedges

▲ 4 ears of corn, husks and silk removed, halved crosswise

▲ 1 large onion, thickly sliced

3 large garlic cloves, chopped

▲ 1 cup reduced-sodium chicken broth

3 tablespoons lemon juice

2 tablespoons unsalted butter, cut into pieces

4 fresh oregano sprigs

¼ teaspoon salt

¼ teaspoon black pepper

⅛ teaspoon cayenne

▲ 16 littleneck clams, scrubbed

▲ 16 mussels, scrubbed and debearded

▲ 2 (1¼-pound) live lobsters

1 Preheat grill to medium-high or prepare medium-high fire.

2 Toss together potatoes, corn, onion, garlic, broth, lemon juice, butter, oregano, salt, black pepper, and cayenne in large, deep disposable foil pan. Cover pan tightly with foil and place on grill rack. Grill, covered, until corn and onion are almost tender, about 20 minutes.

3 Remove pan from grill; carefully open foil to avoid steam. Arrange clams and mussels on top of vegetables in even layer. Set lobsters on top and cover pan tightly with foil. Return pan to grill rack. Grill, covered, until potatoes are tender, lobsters are cooked through, and clams and mussels are opened 20–25 minutes. Carefully open foil. Discard any clams and mussels that do not open. With kitchen scissors, cut lobsters lengthwise in half.

PER SERVING (½ lobster, 4 clams, 4 mussels, 8 potato wedges, 2 pieces of corn, and about ¼ cup broth): 489 Cal, 10 g Total Fat, 4 g Sat Fat, 0 g Trans Fat, 109 mg Chol, 689 mg Sod, 62 g Carb, 7 g Sugar, 7 g Fib, 40 g Prot, 144 mg Calc.

ALL AMERICAN

When the first colonists arrived in New England, they saw Native Americans baking clams and other shellfish over hot stones that were covered with seaweed. Preparing an old-fashioned clambake on a backyard grill is reminiscent of those early years.

MUSSELS IN SPICY TOMATO BROTH

SERVES 6

6 large garlic cloves, peeled

¼ teaspoon red pepper flakes

▲ 1 (28-ounce) can diced tomatoes

1 teaspoon dried thyme

¼ teaspoon salt

1 tablespoon olive oil

▲ 1 small onion, chopped

1 cup dry white wine

▲ 3½ pounds mussels, scrubbed and debearded

6 (2-ounce) slices whole wheat country-style bread, toasted

½ cup chopped fresh parsley

1 To make tomato broth, spray large saucepan with nonstick spray and set over medium heat. Add garlic and cook, stirring, until lightly golden, about 2 minutes. Add pepper flakes and cook, stirring, until fragrant, about 1 minute. Add tomatoes, thyme, and salt. Bring to simmer and cook, stirring occasionally, 10 minutes. Remove saucepan from heat; keep warm.

2 Heat oil in Dutch oven over medium heat. Add onion and cook, stirring, until softened, about 5 minutes. Add wine and bring to boil; add mussels. Cook, covered, until mussels are opened, about 5 minutes. Discard any mussels that do not open.

3 Place 1 slice of toast in each of 6 large shallow soup bowls. With slotted spoon, divide mussels evenly among bowls. Add mussel liquid to tomato broth and bring to simmer. Ladle broth and garlic evenly over mussels; serve sprinkled with parsley.

PER SERVING (1 bowl): 279 Cal, 6 g Total Fat, 1 g Sat Fat, 0 g Trans Fat, 14 mg Chol, 760 mg Sod, 40 g Carb, 9 g Sugar, 4 g Fib, 15 g Prot, 165 mg Calc.

★ **FYI** ★ To start the meal off, serve a sliced white mushroom, radicchio, and baby arugula salad dressed with balsamic vinegar and a pinch each of salt and dried oregano.

RICH CHICKEN AND MATZO BALL SOUP

7 PointsPlus® value
PER SERVING

1 To make soup, put chicken in large pot and add enough cold water to cover. Bring to boil, skimming off foam that rises to surface.

2 Add carrots, celery, onion, garlic, bay leaves, salt, and pepper to pot. Reduce heat and simmer, partially covered, 1 hour 20 minutes. With slotted spoon, transfer chicken to plate. Let soup cook until reduced to about 8 cups.

3 Meanwhile, to make matzo balls, bring large pot of water to boil; reduce heat to simmer.

4 Whisk together eggs, egg whites, oil, and salt in medium bowl until frothy. Stir in matzo meal and 1 tablespoon of seltzer, adding remaining 1 tablespoon seltzer if mixture seems dry. With damp hands, gently shape matzo mixture into 8 equal balls; lower balls into simmering water. Cook, covered, until matzo balls are tender when pierced with toothpick, about 40 minutes (do not open pot during first 25 minutes of cooking time).

5 Remove skin and bones from chicken and discard. Cut chicken into chunks or tear into pieces; return chicken to soup along with matzo balls. Cook until heated through, about 5 minutes. Remove bay leaves and discard. Ladle soup evenly into 8 shallow soup bowls.

SOUP

1 (3½-pound) chicken, cut up and giblets removed

▲ 4 carrots, cut into 1½-inch lengths

▲ 4 celery stalks, cut into 1½-inch lengths

▲ 1 large onion, chopped

2 large garlic cloves, peeled

2 bay leaves

½ teaspoon salt

¼ teaspoon black pepper

MATZO BALLS

▲ 2 large eggs

▲ 2 large egg whites

2 tablespoons canola oil

¾ teaspoon salt

¾ cup matzo meal

1–2 tablespoons seltzer

PER SERVING (1 bowl): 274 Cal, 8 g Total Fat, 2 g Sat Fat, 0 g Trans Fat, 133 mg Chol, 514 mg Sod, 16 g Carb, 3 g Sugar, 2 g Fib, 33 g Prot, 46 mg Calc.

ALL AMERICAN

Matzo ball soup, also known as Jewish penicillin, is enjoyed year-round in homes and Jewish delicatessens across America. Matzo meal—the base for the matzo balls—is made from ground matzos, unleavened crackers that are traditionally eaten during Passover.

FISHERMAN'S WHARF CHOWDER AND
BOSTON BROWN BREAD, PAGE 156

FISHERMAN'S WHARF CHOWDER

PER SERVING

1 Spray Dutch oven with nonstick spray and set over medium heat. Add kielbasa and cook, stirring, until lightly browned, about 4 minutes. Stir in onion and garlic; cook, stirring, until onion is softened, about 5 minutes.

2 Stir potatoes, tomato, clam juice, wine, thyme, cayenne, and saffron into onion mixture; bring to boil. Reduce heat and simmer, covered, 15 minutes. Add clams and simmer, covered, 3 minutes. Stir in mussels; simmer, covered, until clams and mussels are opened, about 3 minutes longer. Discard any clams and mussels that do not open.

3 Add halibut and shrimp to chowder; cook until halibut and shrimp are opaque in center, about 5 minutes. Ladle chowder evenly into 4 bowls. Serve sprinkled with cilantro.

PER SERVING (1 bowl): 261 Cal, 4 g Total Fat, 1 g Sat Fat, 0 g Trans Fat, 92 mg Chol, 444 mg Sod, 22 g Carb, 5 g Sugar, 3 g Fib, 30 g Prot, 98 mg Calc.

2 ounces turkey kielbasa, sliced

▲ 1 onion, chopped

2 garlic cloves, minced

▲ 2 all-purpose potatoes, scrubbed and diced

▲ 1 large tomato, chopped

1 (8-ounce) bottle clam juice

½ cup dry white wine

½ teaspoon dried thyme

¼ teaspoon cayenne

Pinch saffron threads, crushed

▲ 8 littleneck clams, scrubbed

▲ 8 mussels, scrubbed and debearded

▲ ½ pound halibut fillet, cut into 1-inch chunks

▲ ¼ pound large shrimp, peeled and deveined

2 tablespoons chopped fresh cilantro

★ **FYI** ★ To begin your meal, start off with an orange segment, arugula, and fennel salad dressed with lemon juice.

MANHATTAN CLAM CHOWDER WITH BACON AND POTATOES

SERVES 6

6
PointsPlus®
value

PER SERVING

2 cups water

▲ 24 cherrystone clams, scrubbed

1½ teaspoons olive oil

2 slices turkey bacon, chopped

▲ 2 celery stalks, sliced

▲ 1 onion, chopped

2 garlic cloves, minced

▲ 1 (28-ounce) can crushed
tomatoes

▲ 2 large Yukon Gold potatoes,
peeled and cut into ½-inch dice

½ teaspoon dried oregano

¼ teaspoon black pepper

Pinch red pepper flakes

¼ cup chopped fresh flat-leaf
parsley

1 Bring water to boil in large pot. Add clams and cook, covered, until clams are opened, about 10 minutes. With slotted spoon, transfer clams to large bowl. Discard any clams that do not open. Pour clam liquid through fine sieve set over medium bowl. Add enough water to clam liquid to equal 2½ cups.

2 Heat oil in large nonstick saucepan over medium heat. Add bacon and cook, stirring, until crisp; stir in celery, onion, and garlic; cook until onion is softened, about 5 minutes. Stir in clam liquid, tomatoes, potatoes, oregano, black pepper, and pepper flakes; bring to boil. Simmer, partially covered, until potatoes are tender, about 15 minutes.

3 Meanwhile, remove clams from their shells; discard shells. Chop clams. Stir clams and parsley into chowder; cook until heated through, about 2 minutes.

PER SERVING (about 1¼ cups): 224 Cal, 4 g Total Fat, 1 g Sat Fat, 0 g Trans Fat, 30 mg Chol, 356 mg Sod, 34 g Carb, 3 g Sugar, 6 g Fib, 16 g Prot, 114 mg Calc.

ALL AMERICAN

There are two types of clam chowder: New England and Manhattan. The former is cream-based and somewhat thick, while the latter is tomato-based. Which you prefer is simply a matter of personal taste.

BUTTER-AND-SUGAR-GLAZED CARROTS AND ONIONS

PER SERVING

Combine ingredients in large nonstick skillet and bring to boil. Reduce heat and simmer, covered, shaking pan occasionally, until most of liquid is evaporated, about 20 minutes.Continue cooking, shaking pan often to prevent vegetables from sticking, until vegetables are glazed and golden, about 5 minutes longer.

▲ 1 pint pearl onions, peeled

▲ 6 carrots, cut into ½-inch slices

▲ ½ cup reduced-sodium chicken broth

1 tablespoon sugar

1 tablespoon unsalted butter

½ teaspoon dried savory or thyme

¼ teaspoon salt

⅛ teaspoon black pepper

PER SERVING (about 1 cup). 136 Cal, 3 g Total Fat, 2 g Sat Fat, 0 g Trans Fat, 8 mg Chol, 236 mg Sod, 26 g Carb, 10 g Sugar, 3 g Fib, 3 g Prot, 59 mg Calc.

★ **FYI** ★ To peel fresh pearl onions, bring a saucepan of water to a boil. Add the onions and cook for 1 minute, then drain. With a small knife, cut off the root end, then slip off the outer skin.

HOPPIN' JOHN

SERVES 4 ....

PER SERVING

2 slices turkey bacon, chopped

▲ 1 small onion, chopped

▲ ½ green bell pepper, chopped

▲ 1 celery stalk, chopped

2 garlic cloves, minced

▲ 2 scallions, sliced

⅛ teaspoon red pepper flakes

½ cup long-grain white rice

▲ 1 (10-ounce) package frozen black-eyed peas

▲ 1¼ cups reduced-sodium chicken broth

▲ 1 tomato, seeded and diced

1 Cook bacon in large nonstick skillet over medium heat until crisp. With slotted spoon, transfer bacon to paper towel–lined plate to drain.

2 Wipe skillet clean. Spray skillet with nonstick spray and set over medium heat. Add onion, bell pepper, celery, and garlic; cook, stirring, until onion is softened, about 5 minutes. Stir in scallions and pepper flakes; cook, stirring, 1 minute longer.

3 Stir rice, peas, and broth into vegetable mixture and bring to boil. Reduce heat and simmer, covered, until rice is tender and liquid is absorbed, about 20 minutes. Remove skillet from heat. Serve topped with tomato and bacon.

PER SERVING (about 1 cup): 243 Cal, 3 g Total Fat, 1 g Sat Fat, 0 g Trans Fat, 7 mg Chol, 218 mg Sod, 43 g Carb, 2 g Sugar, 6 g Fib, 13 g Prot, 43 mg Calc.

ALL AMERICAN

Hoppin' John is the South's version of rice and beans. Eating it on New Year's Day is thought to bring prosperity throughout the year. The black-eyed peas are symbolic of a coin that is sometimes added to this dish for some lucky person to find.

BACON, RICE, AND BELL PEPPER PERLOO

1 Spray large nonstick skillet with nonstick spray and set over medium-high heat. Add bacon and cook, stirring, until lightly browned, about 2 minutes. Transfer to plate.

2 Heat oil in skillet over medium heat. Add onion, bell pepper and garlic; cook, stirring, until onion is softened, about 5 minutes. Stir in remaining ingredients and bring to boil. Reduce heat and simmer, covered, until rice is tender and liquid is absorbed, about 20 minutes longer.

PER SERVING (about ½ cup): 171 Cal, 4 g Total Fat, 1 g Sat Fat, 0 g Trans Fat, 7 mg Chol, 400 mg Sod, 28 g Carb, 2 g Sugar, 1 g Fib, 7 g Prot, 14 mg Calc.

3 slices Canadian bacon, chopped

1 tablespoon olive oil

▲ 1 small red onion, chopped

▲ 1 small green bell pepper, chopped

2 garlic cloves, minced

1 cup long-grain white rice

▲ 4 plum tomatoes, chopped

▲ 1¾ cups reduced-sodium chicken broth

½ teaspoon salt

¼ teaspoon black pepper

Pinch cayenne

ALL AMERICAN

Whether called perloo, perlew, pilau, plaw, pullao, pilaf, or perlow, this tasty rice dish is appreciated all across America. This rendition is native to Charleston, South Carolina, where rice was once its primary export and the maker of many a fortune.

FARMERS' MARKET TOMATO AND GOAT CHEESE SALAD

▲ 2 bunches arugula (about ½ pound total)

2 tablespoons extra-virgin olive oil

2 teaspoons lemon juice

½ teaspoon salt

▲ 4 heirloom tomatoes, sliced

▲ 1 cup yellow grape or cherry tomatoes, halved

▲ 1 cup red cherry tomatoes, halved

2 teaspoons red wine vinegar

⅓ cup crumbled soft goat cheese

1 tablespoon snipped fresh chives

¼ teaspoon black pepper

1 Toss together arugula, 1 tablespoon of oil, the lemon juice, and ¼ teaspoon of salt in large bowl. Pile on serving plate.

2 Gently toss together tomatoes, remaining 1 tablespoon oil, the vinegar, and remaining ¼ teaspoon salt in same large bowl. Spoon tomato mixture on top of arugula. Sprinkle with goat cheese, chives, and pepper.

PER SERVING (⅙ of salad): 93 Cal, 7 g Total Fat, 2 g Sat Fat, 0 g Trans Fat, 3 mg Chol, 241 mg Sod, 7 g Carb, 4 g Sugar, 2 g Flb, 4 g Prot, 85 mg Calc.

★ **FYI** ★ Turn this summertime salad into a meal by serving it with grilled arctic char. One cooked 3-ounce arctic char fillet per serving will increase the **PointsPlus** value by **4.**

FARMERS' MARKET TOMATO AND GOAT CHEESE SALAD

WHOLE WHEAT–BLUEBERRY GRIDDLE CAKES

SERVES 4

PER SERVING

¾ cup white whole wheat flour

1 tablespoon granulated sugar

1 teaspoon baking powder

¼ teaspoon baking soda

¼ teaspoon salt

¾ cup low-fat buttermilk

▲ 2 large egg whites

2 teaspoons canola oil

▲ 1½ cups fresh blueberries

2 tablespoons sliced almonds, toasted

1 tablespoon confectioners' sugar

1 Whisk together flour, granulated sugar, baking powder, baking soda, and salt in medium bowl. Whisk together buttermilk, egg whites, and oil in small bowl. Add buttermilk mixture to flour mixture, stirring just until flour mixture is moistened. Stir in 1 cup of blueberries just until combined.

2 Spray nonstick griddle or large skillet with nonstick spray and set over medium heat until drop of water sizzles in pan. Pour scant ¼ cupfuls of batter onto griddle. Cook until bubbles begin to appear and edges of pancakes look dry, about 3 minutes. Turn pancakes over and cook until puffed and browned on second side, about 2 minutes longer. Transfer to plate and keep warm. Repeat with remaining batter, making total of 8 pancakes.

3 Place 2 pancakes on each of 4 plates. Sprinkle each serving with ½ tablespoon of almonds and 2 tablespoons of remaining blueberries. Dust with confectioners' sugar.

PER SERVING (1 plate): 207 Cal, 5 g Total Fat, 1 g Sat Fat, 0 g Trans Fat, 2 mg Chol, 438 mg Sod, 35 g Carb, 13 g Sugar, 5 g Fib, 7 g Prot, 90 mg Calc.

★ **FYI** ★ Whether called griddlecakes, flapjacks, hoecakes, johnnycakes, crespelle, crêpes, blintzes, palascinta, or latkes, pancakes are beloved round the world. They can be sweet or savory, served for breakfast, lunch, or dinner, or enjoyed as an appetizer, side dish, or dessert.

OYSTER-BACON DRESSING

1 Preheat oven to 350°F. Spray small baking dish with nonstick spray.

2 Cook bacon in large nonstick skillet over medium heat until crisp. With slotted spoon, transfer bacon to paper towel–lined plate to drain. Crumble bacon.

3 Spray skillet with nonstick spray and set over medium heat. Add onion, carrot, and celery; cook, stirring, until softened, about 5 minutes.

4 Toss together vegetables, bread cubes, egg white, and pepper in large bowl. Drizzle broth over stuffing, tossing until moistened and adding more broth if needed. Add oysters and bacon; stir until mixed well. Spoon dressing into prepared baking dish. Bake until oysters are cooked through and dressing is golden and crusty, about 35 minutes.

2 slices turkey bacon

▲ 1 onion, chopped

▲ 1 carrot, chopped

▲ 1 celery stalk, chopped

4 cups country-style whole wheat bread cubes

▲ 1 large egg white, lightly beaten

¼ teaspoon black pepper

▲ ¾ cup no-salt-added chicken broth

▲ 18 oysters, shucked

PER SERVING (about 1 cup): 251 Cal, 5 g Total Fat, 1 g Sat Fat, 0 g Trans Fat, 34 mg Chol, 569 mg Sod, 43 g Carb, 8 g Sugar, 5 g Fib, 15 g Prot, 181 mg Calc.

★ **FYI** ★ This special oyster dressing makes the ideal accompaniment to a Thanksgiving turkey, Christmas ham, or Easter capon.

BOSTON BROWN BREAD

PER SERVING

1 tablespoon unsalted butter, softened

½ cup rye flour

½ cup whole wheat flour

½ cup yellow cornmeal

1 teaspoon baking soda

½ teaspoon salt

1 cup low-fat buttermilk

⅓ cup light (mild) molasses

Grated zest of ½ orange

½ cup dried currants

1 Grease inside of clean 1-pound coffee can or pudding mold (about 4 cups) with butter.

2 Whisk together rye flour, whole wheat flour, cornmeal, baking soda, and salt in large bowl. Stir in buttermilk, molasses, and orange zest until blended. Stir in currants.

3 Pour batter into prepared can (it should be about ⅔ full). Tightly cover can with sheet of foil and secure with rubber band or kitchen string. Set can in large pot and add enough boiling hot water to come about halfway up side of can. Cover pot and bring to boil. Reduce heat and steam 2 hours, adding additional water, if needed.

4 Wearing oven mitts or with jar lifter, remove can from pot; carefully remove foil. Let bread cool about 5 minutes, then invert can onto wire rack and lift off can. Cut bread into 12 slices and serve hot.

PER SERVING (1 slice): 117 Cal, 1 g Total Fat, 1 g Sat Fat, 0 g Trans Fat, 3 mg Chol, 228 mg Sod, 25 g Carb, 12 g Sugar, 2 g Fib, 2 g Prot, 61 mg Calc.

ALL AMERICAN

In New England, colonists often enjoyed Boston baked beans for their Saturday night supper. As people prospered, Boston brown bread was added to the table. This dark, moist, steamed bread was similar to the rye and Indian corn bread the Native Americans cooked. Nowadays, Boston brown bread is still served with baked beans, especially in Boston.

SWEET POTATO BISCUITS

PER SERVING

1 Preheat oven to 425°F.

2 Whisk together all-purpose flour, white whole wheat flour, brown sugar, baking powder, salt, and baking soda in large bowl. With pastry blender or 2 knives used scissor-fashion, cut in butter until mixture resembles coarse crumbs.

3 Whisk together sweet potato and milk in small bowl until smooth. Add sweet potato mixture to flour mixture, stirring just until flour mixture is moistened.

4 Lightly flour work surface. Turn dough out onto surface and gently knead 10 times or until smooth. (The dough will be soft and wet.) With floured rolling pin, roll out dough to form 8-inch square. With floured knife, cut dough crosswise into 4 equal strips, then cut across into 4 equal pieces, making total of 16 biscuits.

5 Transfer biscuits to ungreased baking sheet. Bake until golden brown, 12–15 minutes. Serve warm or at room temperature.

PER SERVING (1 biscuit): 73 Cal, 2 g Total Fat, 1 g Sat Fat, 0 g Trans Fat, 6 mg Chol, 229 mg Sod, 11 g Carb, 2 g Sugar, 1 g Fib, 2 g Prot, 27 mg Calc.

1 cup all-purpose flour

1 cup white whole wheat flour

1 tablespoon packed brown sugar

2 teaspoons baking powder

¾ teaspoon salt

½ teaspoon baking soda

3 tablespoons cold unsalted butter, cut into pieces

▲ 1 cup mashed cooked sweet potato (about 8 ounces)

▲ ½ cup fat-free milk

★ **FYI** ★ In the 1700s, the sweet potato—a member of the morning glory family—was discovered in Louisiana by Dutch explorer Antoine Le Page du Pratz. For marketing purposes, sweet potatoes are often called yams, but they are not yams at all.

**SPICED ORANGES WITH
SEA SALT AND MINT, PAGE 171**

SWEET 'N' SALTY

★ LIGHT BITES AND SNACKS ★

CHICKEN SKEWERS WITH
SWEET AND SALTY PB SAUCE

PointsPlus value

PER SERVING

SERVES 4

1 Soak 4 (12-inch) bamboo skewers in water
30 minutes.

2 Combine 4 tablespoons of orange juice, the salt,
and pepper in medium bowl. Add chicken and toss to
coat evenly. Let stand at room temperature, turning
occasionally, 10 minutes.

3 Meanwhile, stir together marmalade, peanut
butter, and remaining 1 tablespoon orange juice in
serving bowl.

4 Spray ridged grill pan with nonstick spray and set
over medium heat. Thread chicken onto skewers,
leaving chicken as flat as possible. Place chicken in
grill pan and cook, turning once, until cooked through,
about 5 minutes. Sprinkle with cilantro and serve with
dipping sauce.

PER SERVING (1 skewer and generous 1 tablespoon sauce): 129 Cal,
4 g Fat, 1 g Sat Fat, 0 g Trans Fat, 31 mg Chol, 162 mg Sod, 11 g Carb, 8 g sugar,
0 g Fib, 12 g Prot, 8 Calc.

5 tablespoons orange juice

¼ teaspoon kosher salt

Pinch black pepper

▲ 4 (2-ounce) slices thin-sliced
skinless chicken breast cutlet

3 tablespoons sweet orange
marmalade

1 tablespoon chunky natural
peanut butter

1 tablespoon chopped fresh
cilantro

★ **FYI** ★ Enjoy this tasty bite with long spears of unpeeled cucumber for some refreshing crunch.

SWEET AND SALTY COCONUT SHRIMP

SERVES 4

PER SERVING

½ cup flaked sweetened coconut

⅛ teaspoon salt

▲ 12 large shrimp (about ½ pound), peeled and deveined

2 tablespoons Dijon mustard

1 Preheat oven to 350°F.

2 Spread coconut in shallow baking pan. Toast, stirring twice, until golden brown, about 7 minutes. Transfer coconut to plate. Increase oven temperature to 400°F.

3 Sprinkle salt over shrimp. Put mustard in small bowl. Dip each shrimp into mustard to coat; put on small baking sheet in single layer.

4 Bake until shrimp are just opaque throughout, 3–5 minutes. Roll each shrimp in coconut to coat. Serve hot.

PER SERVING (3 shrimp): 72 Cal, 3 g Fat, 3 g Sat Fat, 0 g Trans Fat, 32 mg Chol, 320 mg Sod, 7 g Carb, 4 g sugar, 1 g Fib, 4 g Prot, 8 Calc.

★ **FYI** ★ To turn these delectable shrimp into a light meal, serve them with a chopped salad of red bell pepper, cucumber, tomatoes, and zucchini.

SWEET AND SALTY COCONUT SHRIMP
AND CHICKEN SKEWERS WITH
SWEET AND SALTY PB SAUCE, PAGE 161

HONEY, SALTED FRUIT, AND NUT MIX

SERVES 16

PER SERVING

1 cup whole natural almonds

½ cup shelled raw sunflower seeds

1 tablespoon honey

¼ teaspoon kosher salt

⅛ teaspoon vanilla extract

¼ cup dried tart cherries, chopped

¼ cup dried California apricots, cut into thirds

1 tablespoon sesame seeds

1 Preheat oven to 350°F.

2 Combine almonds and sunflower seeds in medium bowl. Spray with nonstick spray; toss and spray again. Stir in honey, salt, and vanilla. Spread in single layer on large heavy baking sheet. Bake until nuts are golden brown and shiny, about 13 minutes, stirring halfway through baking time. Let mixture cool completely on baking sheet. Transfer to medium bowl.

3 Stir cherries, apricots, and sesame seeds into nut mixture. Store in airtight container up to 1 week.

PER SERVING (2 tablespoons): 119 Cal, 8 g Fat, 1 g Sat Fat, 0 g Trans Fat, 0 mg Chol, 42 mg Sod, 9 g Carb, 4 g sugar, 3 g Fib, 4 g Prot, 42 Calc.

★ **FYI** ★ Salt 101: Salt is a mineral that is comprised of sodium and chloride. It is one of the four basic tastes, along with bitter, sweet, and sour. All through time, salt has been essential to the preservation of food. It also brings out the flavor in foods, helps to retard food from spoiling, and strengthens the gluten in yeast breads.

SALTY BROWN SUGAR AND THYME-GLAZED PECANS

PER SERVING

1 Preheat oven to 400°F. Line large heavy baking sheet with foil and spray with nonstick spray.

2 Combine water, brown sugar, thyme, salt, and cayenne in small nonstick skillet over medium heat. Cook, stirring often, until sugar is dissolved, about 2 minutes. Remove skillet from heat; add pecans and turbinado sugar; toss until coated evenly.

3 Spread pecans in single layer on prepared baking sheet. Bake, stirring and turning pan around halfway through baking time, until pecans are deep golden brown, about 12 minutes. Let cool completely on baking sheet on wire rack.

4 Remove pecans from foil and separate any that are stuck together. Store in airtight container up to 1 week.

PER SERVING (generous 1 tablespoon): 66 Cal, 6 g Fat, 1 g Sat Fat, 0 g Trans Fat, 0 mg Chol, 40 mg Sod, 3 g Carb, 2 g sugar, 1 g Fib, 1 g Prot, 7 Calc.

1 tablespoon water

1 tablespoon packed brown sugar

¼ teaspoon fresh thyme leaves or ⅛ teaspoon dried thyme, crumbled

¼ teaspoon kosher salt

Pinch cayenne

1 cup pecans

1 tablespoon turbinado (raw) sugar

ALL AMERICAN

The pecan tree is the only major nut tree that is indigenous to North America. The word "pecan" is a Native American word that describes all nuts that require a stone to crack them open. It is believed that the Native Americans were the first to cultivate pecan trees. By the 18th century, English settlers, had also planted these trees. For information about turbinado sugar, see page 167.

CARAMEL POPCORN WITH CASHEWS AND GINGER

SERVES 10

PER SERVING

▲ 6 cups air-popped popcorn (about ¼ cup unpopped)

¼ cup coarsely chopped salted roasted cashews

1½ teaspoons minced crystallized ginger

⅛ teaspoon baking soda

½ cup sugar

⅓ cup light corn syrup

1 tablespoon unsalted butter, softened

½ teaspoon fine sea salt or table salt

1 Preheat oven to 325°F. Spray large heavy baking sheet with nonstick spray.

2 Spread popcorn and cashews in single layer on prepared baking sheet. Combine ginger and baking soda in small bowl.

3 Combine sugar, corn syrup, butter, and salt in small heavy saucepan over medium-low heat. Cook, stirring constantly, until sugar is dissolved. Increase heat to medium-high and bring to boil; boil until temperature registers 250°F (hard-ball stage) on candy thermometer.

4 Remove pan from heat and stir in ginger–baking soda mixture. Pour sugar mixture over popcorn and cashews and toss with pancake spatula until coated evenly. (Be careful as sugar mixture is very hot.)

5 Bake popcorn mixture 10 minutes; stir and turn with pancake spatula to ensure all popcorn is coated. Bake, stirring twice, until golden brown, about 10 minutes longer. Stir again and let cool completely on baking sheet on wire rack. Break up any clumps of popcorn. Popcorn can be stored in airtight container at room temperature up to 1 week.

PER SERVING (⅔ cup): 146 Cal, 4 g Fat, 2 g Sat Fat, 0 g Trans Fat, 4 mg Chol, 207 mg Sod, 29 g Carb, 14 g sugar, 1 g Fib, 2 g Prot, 4 Calc.

★ **FYI** ★ For the best results here, use freshly popped corn. For information about sea salt, see page 169.

MAKE IT SALTY, MAKE IT SWEET

Besides the most common salts and sugars is a colorful, flavorful array that can brighten up just about any dish with a mere sprinkle.

★ SALTS ★

NAME	DESCRIPTION	BEST USES
Fleur de sel (flower of salt)	is highly prized and appreciated for its fresh, briny flavor. It is hand-harvested by workers who remove the crystals that form on the surface of salt evaporation ponds off the coast of Brittany in France.	sprinkled on rolls and cookies
Hawaiian sea salt	also known as Alaea sea salt, contains a mineral known as alae (volcanic baked red clay), which is added to this salt to give it its distinctive reddish hue. This coarse textured salt has a suble flavor that has an earthy quality.	Hawaiian and Island-style pork and beef dishes, kebabs
Himalayan pink salt	contains 84 trace minerals and is mined from ancient salt beds formed over 200 million years ago. This salt comes in various hues, from white to pink to clear red.	sprinkled over finished dishes such as broiled fish
Sel gris (gray salt)	is a moist, unrefined salt found along the Brittany coast in France. It has a natural light gray color from the absorption of minerals from the clay that lines the salt ponds.	stews, braises, over ice cream, fudge sauce
Smoked salts	such as alderwood, hickory, mesquite and applewood, are fairly new to the market. Their smoky flavor is an easy way to add smoke flavor to dishes. High-quality smoked salts are made by allowing the salt to absorb the natural flavor through a slow smoking process. There are only two companies in the U.S. that produce authentic smoked salt: Saltworks and Smokehouse Salt Company.	sprinkled over finished dishes, such as grilled meats, chicken, pork, eggplant, corn, zucchini

★ SUGARS ★

NAME	DESCRIPTION	BEST USES
Agave nectar	is gaining in popularity. It is most often extracted from the blue agave plant and is primarily produced in Mexico. It is about one and a half times sweeter than sugar or honey.	iced tea, muffins, over pancakes and waffles
Superfine sugar	also called bar sugar and caster sugar, has the finest granulation of any sugar. It's appreciated for the fact that it dissolves instantly.	drinks, meringues
Turbinado sugar	also known as raw sugar, is what remains during the sugar refining process just before the molasses is removed. It is tan-colored and lightly molasses flavored.	sprinkled over pies, cookies, and other baked goods

PUMPKIN SEED–BACON
PRALINE

PUMPKIN SEED-BACON PRALINE

4
PointsPlus®
value

PER SERVING

1 Preheat oven to 350°F. Spray large heavy baking sheet with nonstick spray.

2 Spread pumpkin seeds in single layer on prepared baking sheet. Bake, stirring twice, until golden brown, about 7 minutes. Let cool on baking sheet on wire rack. Push seeds close together to form 7-inch round.

3 Cook bacon in small nonstick skillet over medium-high heat until crisp. With slotted spoon, transfer to paper towel–lined plate to drain. Crumble bacon and sprinkle evenly over pumpkin seeds.

4 Combine sugar, water, corn syrup, and salt in medium heavy saucepan over medium heat. Cook, stirring, until sugar is dissolved. Increase heat to high and bring to boil, washing down side of pan with wet pastry brush to dissolve any sugar crystals. Boil, without stirring, until caramel is dark amber, swirling pan toward end of cooking.

5 Immediately pour caramel over pumpkin seed mixture in circular motion to coat evenly. If needed, move seed mixture around with fork to ensure pumpkin seed mixture is completely coated. (Be careful as the fork can get very hot.) Let praline stand until cooled and hardened, about 15 minutes. Break into 1- to 2-inch pieces. Store in airtight container up to 1 week.

¾ cup shelled pumpkin seeds

1 slice bacon, cut crosswise into ¼-inch strips

¾ cup sugar

2 tablespoons water

1 tablespoon light corn syrup

¼ teaspoon kosher salt

PER SERVING (scant ¼ cup): 129 Cal, 6 g Fat, 1 g Sat Fat, 0 g Trans Fat, 1 mg Chol, 87 mg Sod, 18 g Carb, 14 g sugar, 1 g Fib, 4 g Prot, 6 Calc.

★ **FYI** ★ *Table salt* is fine salt that is commonly used for day-to-day cooking. It is treated so that it will easily pour without clumping. *Kosher salt* is made of large, irregular crystals and is the salt of choice for many cooks, as it is easy to sprinkle and has a mild, salty flavor. *Sea salt* is produced by evaporating seawater. It is available fine and coarse ground.

STRAWBERRIES WITH SALT AND LEMON-FLAVORED SUGAR

SERVES 4 | 20 MIN

2 tablespoons sugar

1 teaspoon grated lemon zest

¼ teaspoon kosher salt

⅛ teaspoon black pepper

▲ 1 (1-pound) container strawberries, hulled and sliced

Combine sugar, lemon zest, salt, and pepper in medium bowl, stirring and pressing lemon zest into sugar with spoon. Add strawberries to sugar mixture; let stand until sugar is dissolved and juices are released, about 10 minutes. Serve at room temperature.

PER SERVING (generous ½ cup): 50 Cal, 0 g Fat, 0 g Sat Fat, 0 g Trans Fat, 0 mg Chol, 121 mg Sod, 13 g Carb, 10 g sugar, 2 g Fib, 1 g Prot, 18 Calc.

SPICED ORANGES WITH SEA SALT AND MINT

PointsPlus value

PER SERVING

1 With sharp knife, cut off slice from top and bottom of oranges. Stand fruit upright. Cut off peel and white pith, cutting from top to bottom, turning fruit as you go. Cut oranges crosswise into rounds about ⅜ inch thick. Remove and discard any seeds. Arrange orange slices in overlapping circles on serving plate.

2 Stir together sugar, salt, and allspice in cup; sprinkle over oranges. Refrigerate, covered, until chilled, 1–2 hours. Thinly slice mint leaves; sprinkle over oranges.

▲ **4 large navel oranges**

1 tablespoon sugar

¼ teaspoon coarse sea salt or kosher salt

¼ teaspoon ground allspice

6 fresh mint leaves

PER SERVING (¾ cup): 76 Cal, 0 g Fat, 0 g Sat Fat, 0 g Trans Fat, 0 mg Chol, 121 mg Sod, 20 g Carb, 14 g sugar, 3 g Fib, 1 g Prot, 61 Calc.

★ **FYI** ★ These sweet, salty, warmly spiced oranges are a great accompaniment to grilled skinless boneless chicken breasts and grilled zucchini (one 3-ounce cooked chicken breast per serving will increase the **PointsPlus** value by **3**).

BUTTERSCOTCH-CLEMENTINE SUNDAES

SERVES 4 ....

⅓ cup packed dark brown sugar

▲ 2 tablespoons fat-free half-and-half

1 tablespoon agave nectar or light corn syrup

1 tablespoon unsalted butter, softened

¼ teaspoon kosher salt

¼ teaspoon vanilla extract

▲ 4 small clementines

1 pint vanilla fat-free ice cream

1 Combine brown sugar, half-and-half, agave nectar, butter, and salt in medium saucepan and set over low heat. Cook, whisking constantly, until brown sugar is dissolved and butter is melted.

2 Increase heat to medium and cook, whisking constantly, just until heated through, about 1 minute. Transfer sauce to small glass measure; stir in vanilla and let cool to room temperature.

3 To assemble sundaes, peel clementines, separate into halves, and cut each half crosswise into thirds to form half-moon shapes. Separate into individual pieces (segments). Place ½-cup scoop of ice cream in each of 4 dessert or sundae dishes; top evenly with sauce and clementines. Serve at once.

PER SERVING (½ cup ice cream, scant 2 tablespoons sauce, and 1 clementine): 245 Cal, 5 g Fat, 3 g Sat Fat, 0 g Trans Fat, 13 mg Chol, 186 mg Sod, 53 g Carb, 41 g sugar, 5 g Fib, 3 g Prot, 132 Calc.

★ **FYI** ★ The sauce can be refrigerated in a covered container up to 1 week. For the best flavor, let it come to room temperature before serving. For information about agave nectar, see page 167.

CHOCOLATE CHIP COOKIES WITH SALTED PEANUTS

2
PointsPlus®
value

PER SERVING

1 Place oven racks in upper and lower thirds of oven and preheat oven to 350°F. Spray 2 large baking sheets with nonstick spray.

2 Process oats in food processor until finely ground. Add flour, baking soda, and salt; pulse until combined. With electric mixer on low speed, beat butter, brown sugar, egg, and vanilla in large bowl until smooth and creamy. Gradually add flour mixture, beating just until blended. Combine 1 tablespoon of chocolate chips and 1 tablespoon of peanuts in cup. Stir remaining chocolate chips and peanuts into dough.

3 Roll level tablespoonfuls of dough into balls. Place 2 inches apart on prepared baking sheets, making total of 24 cookies. With bottom of glass, press each ball to form ⅜-inch-thick cookie. Sprinkle evenly with reserved chocolate-peanut mixture, pressing lightly so it adheres.

4 Bake cookies until lightly browned along edges, 9–11 minutes, switching and rotating baking sheets halfway through baking time. Let cool on baking sheets on wire racks about 1 minute. With pancake spatula, transfer cookies to racks and let cool completely. Store in airtight container up to 3 days.

½ cup quick-cooking (not instant) oats

1 cup all-purpose flour

½ teaspoon baking soda

¼ teaspoon fine table or sea salt

4 tablespoons unsalted butter, melted and cooled

¾ cup packed dark brown sugar

1 large egg

¼ teaspoon vanilla extract

¼ cup mini semisweet chocolate chips

¼ cup chopped salted roasted peanuts

PER SERVING (1 cookie): 90 Cal, 4 g Fat, 2 g Sat Fat, 0 g Trans Fat, 14 mg Chol, 68 mg Sod, 13 g Carb, 8 g sugar, 1 g Fib, 1 g Prot, 9 Calc.

SWEET AND SALTY CHOCOLATE TRUFFLES

MAKES 36

PER SERVING

8 ounces semisweet chocolate, finely chopped

▲ ¼ cup fat-free half-and-half

2 tablespoons packed light brown sugar

1 tablespoon unsalted butter

¾ teaspoon fleur de sel or other coarse salt

½ teaspoon vanilla extract

3 tablespoons unsweetened cocoa

1 Fill medium saucepan with 1½ inches of water and bring to bare simmer. Combine chocolate, half-and-half, brown sugar, butter, and ¼ teaspoon of salt in heatproof bowl; set over barely simmering water. Cook, stirring often, until chocolate and butter are melted and mixture is smooth.

2 Remove bowl from saucepan; stir in vanilla. Scrape chocolate mixture into medium bowl; let cool to room temperature. Cover bowl with plastic wrap; refrigerate until chocolate mixture is firm, at least 2 hours or up to 2 days.

3 Place cocoa on small plate. Working quickly, roll rounded measuring teaspoonfuls of chocolate mixture into 1-inch balls, then roll in cocoa to coat, shaking off excess, making total of 36 truffles. If serving immediately, sprinkle truffles evenly with remaining salt. Or store between layers of wax paper in covered container and refrigerate up to 1 week. Let truffles stand at room temperature about 15 minutes before serving; sprinkle with salt.

PER SERVING (1 truffle): 40 Cal, 2 g Fat, 1 g Sat Fat, 0 g Trans Fat, 1 mg Chol, 42 mg Sod, 5 g Carb, 4 g sugar, 0 g Fib, 1 g Prot, 4 Calc.

★ **FYI** ★ For information about fleur de sel, see page 167.

SUPER REFRESHING LIMEADE

SERVES 6

1 Grate 1 teaspoon zest from lime and thinly slice lime. Place zest in cup and cover with folded damp paper towel.

2 Combine cool water, sliced lime, ¾ cup of sugar, and ¼ teaspoon of salt in large saucepan over high heat. Bring to boil, stirring often, until sugar is dissolved. Remove saucepan from heat and let stand, covered, 5 minutes.

3 Pour sugar syrup through coarse strainer into pitcher or glass measure; stir in lime juice. Let come to room temperature.

4 Mix together reserved zest and remaining 1 teaspoon sugar and ⅛ teaspoon salt on small plate. Fill small bowl with water. Dip rims of 6 tall thin glasses into water, then dip into zest mixture to coat rims. Add ice to glasses and top with limeade.

1 lime

3½ cups cool water

¾ cup + 1 teaspoon sugar

¼ + ⅛ teaspoon kosher salt

1 cup lime juice (about 8 limes)

PER SERVING (scant 1 cup limeade): 75 Cal, 0 g Fat, 0 g Sat Fat, 0 g Trans Fat, 0 mg Chol, 127 mg Sod, 23 g Carb, 19 g sugar, 0 g Fib, 0 g Prot, 13 Calc.

SWEET

BIG BLUEBERRY PIE, PAGE 180

★ PIES ★

Apple and Brown Sugar Crumb Pie, 179

Big Blueberry Pie, 180

Lemon Chess Pie, 181

Brandy-Soaked Apple–Dried Currant Crisp, 182

Sweet Potato Pie, 184

Peach-Raspberry Crisp, 185

Dropped Biscuit Berry Cobbler, 187

Black and Blue Berry Slump, 188

Bartlett Pear–Honey Pandowdy, 190

★ CAKES ★

Dried Fig, Walnut, and Rum Cake, 191

Cranberry-Pecan Quick Bread, 193

New York Cheesecake, 194

Orange-and-Rosemary-Scented Strawberry Shortcake, 195

★ PUDDINGS ★

Baked Pumpkin Custards with Sugared Walnuts, 196

Indian Pudding, 198

Tapioca Pudding with Spiced Cherry and Apricot Compote, 199

★ FRUIT DESSERTS ★

Easy Peach Melba, 201

Lemon-Lime Sherbet, 202

★ COOKIES ★

Rhubarb-Raspberry Oatmeal Bars, 203

Moravian Spice Cookies, 204

APPLE AND BROWN SUGAR CRUMB PIE

PER SERVING

1 To make crust, whisk together flour and salt in medium bowl. With fork, stir in oil, then stir in ice water, 1 tablespoon at a time, until dough is moist enough to hold together. Gather dough into ball, then flatten into disk. Wrap in plastic wrap and refrigerate at least 30 minutes or up to overnight.

2 Preheat oven to 375°F.

3 To make filling, melt butter in large nonstick skillet over medium-high heat. Add apples, granulated sugar, cinnamon, and nutmeg; cook, stirring, until apples are softened, about 10 minutes. Remove skillet from heat and let apple mixture cool slightly.

4 To make topping, with fork, stir together topping ingredients in medium bowl until blended well. Squeeze mixture to form loose ball.

5 Lightly flour work surface. With floured rolling pin, roll out dough to 12-inch round; ease into 9-inch pie plate, pressing it against side of pie plate. Spoon filling into pie shell. Break topping into small pieces and sprinkle evenly over filling.

6 Place pie on baking sheet to catch any overflow. Bake until filling is bubbly and topping is golden, about 30 minutes. Let cool on wire rack.

PER SERVING (¹⁄₁₂ of pie): 218 Cal, 10 g Total Fat, 1 g Sat Fat, 0 g Trans Fat, 2 mg Chol, 49 mg Sod, 33 g Carb, 17 g Sugar, 2 g Fib, 2 g Prot, 10 mg Calc.

CRUST

1¼ cups all-purpose flour

¼ teaspoon salt

5 tablespoons canola oil

1–3 tablespoons ice water

FILLING

1 tablespoon unsalted butter

▲ 5 large Granny Smith apples, peeled, cored, and cut into ¼-inch slices

½ cup granulated sugar

½ teaspoon ground cinnamon

¼ teaspoon ground nutmeg

TOPPING

½ cup all-purpose flour

2 tablespoons rolled (old-fashioned) oats

2 tablespoons canola oil

1 tablespoon packed brown sugar

★ **FYI** ★ Although ground nutmeg is readily available in the spice aisle, it is better to purchase whole nutmeg and grate it each time you need it. The reason is that once ground, nutmeg quickly loses its flavor. No need for a special nutmeg grater; a Microplane grater does a great job.

BIG BLUEBERRY PIE

SERVES 12

CRUST

2 cups all-purpose flour

⅓ cup ice water

½ teaspoon salt

½ cup (1 stick) cold unsalted butter, cut into pieces

1 tablespoon sugar

FILLING

▲ 6 cups fresh or frozen blueberries

1 tablespoon lemon juice

¾ cup sugar

¼ cup cornstarch

1 To make crust, whisk together ⅓ cup of flour and the ice water in small bowl until smooth. Stir together remaining 1⅔ cups flour and the salt in large bowl. With pastry blender or 2 knives used scissor-fashion, cut in butter until mixture resembles coarse crumbs. Add flour-water mixture, tossing with fork until dough is moist enough to hold together. Divide dough in half. Shape each piece of dough into disk; wrap each disk in plastic wrap. Refrigerate at least 30 minutes or up to overnight.

2 Preheat oven to 425°F.

3 To make filling, toss together blueberries and lemon juice in large bowl. Add sugar and cornstarch, tossing until mixed well.

4 On lightly floured work surface with floured rolling pin, roll out one disk of dough to 11-inch round; ease into 9-inch pie plate, pressing it against side of pie plate. Spoon filling into pie shell.

5 Roll out remaining disk of dough to 11-inch round; cut into 9 strips and place over filling to form lattice crust. Trim excess pastry; fold edge under and form decorative edge. Brush crust with water and sprinkle with remaining 1 tablespoon sugar. Place pie on baking sheet to catch any overflow.

6 Bake pie 20 minutes. Reduce oven temperature to 350°F and bake until crust is golden brown and filling is bubbly, 45–60 minutes longer. Let cool completely on wire rack.

PER SERVING (¹⁄₁₂ of pie): 229 Cal, 8 g Total Fat, 5 g Sat Fat, 0 g Trans Fat, 20 mg Chol, 3 mg Sod, 39 g Carb, 17 g Sugar, 2 g Fib, 3 g Prot, 10 mg Calc.

LEMON CHESS PIE

1 To make crust, mix together baking mix, cornmeal, and sugar in large bowl. Stir together milk and oil in cup. Add milk mixture to cornmeal mixture, stirring with fork until dough is moist enough to hold together. Turn dough out onto lightly floured work surface and knead 5 times.

2 With floured rolling pin, roll out dough to 11-inch round. Ease dough into 9-inch pie plate, pressing it against side of pie plate. Fold edge of dough over and press against side of pie plate. Freeze 10 minutes.

3 Meanwhile, preheat oven to 375°F.

4 Line pie shell with foil and fill with dried beans or rice. Bake until edge of pie shell is set, about 10 minutes. Remove foil with beans. Bake until pie shell is golden, about 10 minutes. Transfer pie shell to wire rack and let cool 15 minutes.

5 Reduce oven temperature to 350°F.

6 To make filling, whisk together sugar and flour in large bowl until blended. Whisk in eggs. Add remaining ingredients and stir until blended well. Pour filling into pie shell. Cover crust with foil to prevent overbrowning. Bake until filling is set along edge but still jiggly in center, 25–30 minutes (pie will continue to set as it cools). Let cool completely on wire rack.

CRUST

¾ cup reduced-fat buttermilk baking mix

3 tablespoons cornmeal

1 tablespoon sugar

▲ 3 tablespoons fat-free milk

1 tablespoon olive oil

FILLING

1 cup sugar

2 tablespoons all-purpose flour

▲ 3 large eggs

1¼ cups low-fat buttermilk

1 tablespoon grated lemon zest

¼ cup lemon juice

1 tablespoon unsalted butter, melted

1 teaspoon vanilla extract

PER SERVING (⅛ of pie): 239 Cal, 7 g Total Fat, 2 g Sat Fat, 0 g Trans Fat, 86 mg Chol, 333 mg Sod, 41 g Carb, 23 g Sugar, 1 g Fib, 6 g Prot, 93 mg Calc.

ALL AMERICAN

This old-time pie is also known as Jefferson Davis pie and vinegar pie. The custardy filling usually contains vinegar, but here we have enlivened it by substituting fresh lemon zest and juice.

BRANDY-SOAKED APPLE-DRIED CURRANT CRISP

PER SERVING

SERVES 10

⅓ cup dried currants

3 tablespoons brandy or dark rum

¾ cup all-purpose flour

½ cup rolled (old-fashioned) oats

½ cup packed brown sugar

4 tablespoons unsalted butter, melted

1 teaspoon ground cinnamon

▲ 5 Golden Delicious apples, peeled, cored, and sliced

⅓ cup granulated sugar

1 tablespoon lemon juice

Pinch salt

1 Toss together currants and brandy in small bowl; let soak at least 30 minutes or up to 2 hours, stirring occasionally.

2 Preheat oven to 350°F.

3 To make topping, mix together flour, oats, brown sugar, butter, and cinnamon in medium bowl until blended well.

4 Toss together apples, granulated sugar, lemon juice, and salt in large bowl. Spoon into to 9-inch square baking dish or 10-cup casserole dish. Sprinkle currants and any remaining brandy over apples. Sprinkle oat mixture evenly over apples.

5 Bake until top of crisp is golden brown and apples are tender, 45 minutes–1 hour. Transfer to wire rack. Serve warm or at room temperature.

PER SERVING (¹⁄₁₀ of crisp): 224 Cal, 5 g Total Fat, 3 g Sat Fat, 0 g Trans Fat, 12 mg Chol, 18 mg Sod, 43 g Carb, 30 g Sugar, 2 g Fib, 2 g Prot, 25 mg Calc.

BRANDY-SOAKED APPLE–DRIED CURRANT CRISP

SWEET POTATO PIE

PER SERVING

CRUST

1¼ cups all-purpose flour

1 tablespoon sugar

¼ teaspoon salt

3 tablespoons canola oil

2–4 tablespoons ice water

FILLING

1 (15 ½-ounce) can cut yams in light syrup, drained

¾ cup packed dark brown sugar

1 (12-ounce) can fat-free evaporated milk

▲ 2 large eggs

▲ 2 large egg whites

2 tablespoons dark rum or bourbon (optional)

½ teaspoon ground cinnamon

½ teaspoon ground allspice

½ teaspoon salt

¼ teaspoon ground nutmeg

1 To make crust, whisk together flour, sugar, and salt in medium bowl. Stir in oil, then stir in ice water, 1 tablespoon at a time, until dough is moist enough to hold together. Gather dough into ball, then flatten into disk. Wrap in plastic wrap and refrigerate at least 30 minutes or up to overnight.

2 On lightly floured work surface with floured rolling pin, roll out dough to 12-inch round; ease into 10-inch deep-dish pie plate, pressing it against side of pie plate. With fork, prick dough all over and decoratively crimp edge. Freeze 15 minutes.

3 Meanwhile, preheat oven to 375°F.

4 Line pie shell with foil and fill with dried beans or rice. Bake until edge of pie shell is set, about 10 minutes. Remove foil with beans. Bake until pie shell is golden, about 10 minutes longer. Let cool on wire rack 10 minutes.

5 To make filling, with potato masher or electric mixer, mash yams in large bowl until smooth. Stir in remaining filling ingredients until smooth; pour into pie shell.

6 Bake until pie is almost set in center, 40–45 minutes (pie will continue to set as it cools). Let cool completely on wire rack.

PER SERVING (¹⁄₁₂ of pie): 215 Cal, 5 g Total Fat, 1 g Sat Fat, 0 g Trans Fat, 37 mg Chol, 217 mg Sod, 37 g Carb, 20 g Sugar, 2 g Fib, 6 g Prot, 108 mg Calc.

PEACH-RASPBERRY CRISP

SERVES 6

1 Preheat oven to 400°F.

2 Toss together peaches, granulated sugar, and lemon juice in 2-quart baking dish. Sprinkle with raspberries.

3 To make topping, mix together flour, oats, and brown sugar. With your fingertips, rub butter into flour mixture until mixture is crumbly. Sprinkle evenly over peach mixture.

4 Bake until topping is browned and peaches are tender, about 30 minutes.

PER SERVING (⅙ of crisp): 186 Cal, 5 g Total Fat, 3 g Sat Fat, 0 g Trans Fat, 10 mg Chol, 4 mg Sod, 36 g Carb, 24 g Sugar, 6 g Fib, 3 g Prot, 31 mg Calc.

▲ 4 large peaches, unpeeled, pitted and sliced

2 tablespoons granulated sugar

1 tablespoon lemon juice

▲ 2 (6-ounce) containers fresh raspberries

¼ cup all-purpose flour

¼ cup rolled (old-fashioned) oats

¼ cup packed brown sugar

2 tablespoons cold unsalted butter, cut into pieces

★ **FYI** ★ Nectarines work equally well in this fruit crisp. When picking out nectarines or peaches, choose fruit that is fragrant, which will ensure especially delectable fruit when fully ripe.

DROPPED BISCUIT BERRY COBBLER

DROPPED BISCUIT BERRY COBBLER

6
PointsPlus®
value

PER SERVING

1 Preheat oven to 400°F.

2 Stir together ½ cup of sugar, the water, cornstarch, and vanilla in large bowl until sugar is dissolved. Gently stir in peach, raspberries, and blueberries. Spoon into shallow 2-quart baking dish.

3 Whisk together all-purpose flour, white whole wheat flour, remaining ¼ cup sugar, the baking powder, baking soda, and salt in medium bowl. With pastry blender or 2 knives used scissor-fashion, cut in butter until mixture resembles coarse crumbs. Add milk and stir just until thick batter is formed.

4 Drop 8 spoonfuls of batter over fruit, placing evenly.

5 Bake until biscuits are deep golden and juices are bubbly, about 35 minutes. Transfer to wire rack. Serve warm or at room temperature.

PER SERVING (⅛ of cobbler): 220 Cal, 7 g Total Fat, 4 g Sat Fat, 0 g Trans Fat, 16 mg Chol, 190 mg Sod, 40 g Carb, 21 g Sugar, 6 g Fib, 3 g Prot, 52 mg Calc.

¾ cup granulated sugar

⅓ cup water

1 tablespoon cornstarch

1 teaspoon vanilla extract

▲ 1 large peach, unpeeled, pitted and cut into wedges

▲ 3 cups fresh raspberries (about two 6-ounce containers)

▲ 2 cups fresh blueberries (about 1 pint)

½ cup all-purpose flour

½ cup white whole wheat flour

1 teaspoon baking powder

¼ teaspoon baking soda

¼ teaspoon salt

4 tablespoons cold unsalted butter, cut into pieces

½ cup low-fat (1%) milk

★ **FYI** ★ If you like, a fresh nectarine or 3 or 4 fresh apricots can be substituted for the peach.

BLACK AND BLUE BERRY SLUMP

PER SERVING

1 cup all-purpose flour

⅔ cup + 3 tablespoons sugar

1 ¼ teaspoons baking powder

½ teaspoon ground cinnamon

½ teaspoon salt

¼ teaspoon baking soda

½ cup low-fat buttermilk

2 tablespoons unsalted butter, melted

▲ 2 cups fresh blackberries (about two 6-ounce containers)

▲ 2 cups fresh blueberries (about 1 pint)

⅓ cup water

1 tablespoon lemon juice

1 Whisk together flour, 3 tablespoons of sugar, the baking powder, cinnamon, salt, and baking soda in medium bowl. Add buttermilk and butter, stirring until soft, sticky dough forms.

2 Toss together blackberries, blueberries, remaining ⅔ cup sugar, the water, and lemon juice in 10-inch cast-iron or other heavy skillet; bring to boil. Reduce heat and simmer 2 minutes.

3 Drop dough by tablespoonfuls over fruit. Simmer, covered, until toothpick inserted into topping comes out clean, 8–10 minutes. Serve warm.

PER SERVING (⅛ of slump): 179 Cal, 3 g Total Fat, 2 g Sat Fat, 0 g Trans Fat, 8 mg Chol, 289 mg Sod, 38 g Carb, 22 g Sugar, 3 g Fib, 3 g Prot, 51 mg Calc.

ALL AMERICAN

A slump—also called a grunt—is a traditional dessert in New England. It is similar to a cobbler except that it is cooked on top of the stove instead of in the oven. It can be made with almost any fruit, but berries are often the fruit of choice.

BAKE AN AMERICAN PIE

Pies as we know them today are a rather recent addition to food history. The Greeks are believed to have created pie dough around 1200 B.C. A pie was made by wrapping a simple flour-water dough around meat to seal in the juices. In Medieval England, *pyes* were savory; filled with duck, birds, lamb, or beef, singly or in combination and flavored with dried fruit such as currants or dates and black pepper. In time, pies containing one main filling ingredient became more commonplace. The colonists brought time-honored recipes for pies with them to America, but we now know that there was no fruit pie, pecan pie, or pumpkin pie at the first Thanksgiving in 1621. Pumpkin pie, first recorded in a cookbook in 1675 didn't really gain in popularity until the 1800s. An early version of apple pie was eaten in pre-Revolutionary England. It consisted of unsweetened apples encased in an inedible shell.

Other types of fruit pies, known as spoon pies, have become very popular, partly because of their no-fuss nature. Unlike a standard pie that has a crust, most spoon pies (cobblers, grunts, buckles, and crisps, etc) are made up of a fruit filling that is spooned in a baking dish and covered with a topping.

- **Pie** is a baked dessert with a filling and a single bottom crust, a top and bottom crust (called a double-crust pie), a bottom crust and crumb topping, or no bottom crust and a crumb or pastry topping. It can be made in a standard 9-inch pie plate, a deep-dish pie plate, or in individual pie plates.
- **Galette** also known as a rustic pie or crostata, is a free-form pie that is baked in a pie plate or on a baking sheet. The dough is rolled into a round, the fruit filling is spooned into the center and the outer edge of dough is folded over the filling, leaving the center uncovered.
- **Cobbler** This dessert consists of a fruit filling that is spooned into a deep baking dish and covered with rolled out pie dough, cut-out biscuits, or drop biscuits. It is often served with vanilla ice cream.
- **Crisp or Crumble** A fruit filling is spooned into a baking dish and covered with streusel topping. At its simplest, the streusel is made up of flour, brown sugar, spices, and butter that is cut in until the mixture is crumbly. Favored add-ins often include oatmeal, chopped nuts, bread crumbs, or crushed cookies.
- **Grunt** A dessert that dates back to Colonial America, it is a kind of cobbler that is made with berries or fruit and covered with a biscuitlike topping. Traditionally it was steamed over an open fire, but modern-day grunts are baked in a skillet.
- **Pandowdy** A Pandowdy is a deep-dish fruit dessert that is covered with a biscuitlike topping. Partway through the baking, the crust is broken up and pushed into the filling so it can absorb some of the fruit juices. This technique is known as "dowdying."
- **Slump** A Colonial New England deep-dish dessert that often has a top and bottom biscuit-dough crust and is baked in the oven.

★ MAKE MINE À LA MODE! ★

Love your pie, crisp, or slump à la mode—topped with ice cream? Keep the creaminess high and the calories low by reaching for fat-free frozen yogurt or ice cream. Or try a generous spoonful of fat-free or low-fat Greek yogurt sprinkled with turbinado or brown sugar.

BARTLETT PEAR-HONEY PANDOWDY

SERVES 16

PER SERVING

7 Bartlett pears, peeled, cored, and thinly sliced

¼ cup honey

1½ cups + 2 tablespoons all-purpose flour

1 tablespoon lemon juice

¾ teaspoon ground cinnamon

½ teaspoon ground nutmeg

1½ teaspoons baking powder

½ teaspoon salt

⅔ cup sugar

2 large egg whites, lightly beaten

½ cup (1 stick) unsalted butter, melted and cooled

½ cup fat-free milk

1 Preheat oven to 350°F.

2 To make filling, toss together pears and honey in large bowl until coated evenly. Add 2 tablespoons of flour, the lemon juice, cinnamon, and nutmeg; stir until mixed well. Spoon into 2-quart baking dish.

3 To make topping, whisk together remaining 1½ cups flour, the baking powder, and salt in medium bowl. Stir together sugar, egg whites, butter, and milk in another medium bowl. Add milk mixture to flour mixture, stirring just until flour mixture is moistened. Pour over pear mixture and spread evenly.

4 Bake pandowdy until filling is bubbly and top is golden brown, 40–45 minutes. Transfer to wire rack. Serve warm or at room temperature.

PER SERVING (¹⁄₁₆ of pandowdy): 217 Cal, 6 g Total Fat, 4 g Sat Fat, 0 g Trans Fat, 16 mg Chol, 137 mg Sod, 41 g Carb, 24 g Sugar, 5 g Fib, 3 g Prot, 37 mg Calc.

DRIED FIG, WALNUT, AND RUM CAKE

5
PointsPlus®
value

PER SERVING

1 Preheat oven to 325°F. Grease and flour 10-inch tube pan.

2 Toss together walnuts, figs, currants, and ½ cup of flour in medium bowl. Whisk together remaining 1 cup flour, the baking powder, cinnamon, and nutmeg in another medium bowl.

3 With electric mixer on medium speed, beat butter and ¾ cup of sugar and the butter in large bowl until light and fluffy, about 3 minutes. Beat in egg yolks, one at a time, beating well after each addition. Beat in vanilla. Reduce mixer speed to low. Alternately add flour mixture and rum, beginning and ending with flour mixture and beating just until blended. Add walnut mixture, beating just until mixed.

4 Wash and dry beaters. With electric mixer on medium speed, beat egg whites and salt in medium bowl until soft peaks form when beaters are lifted. Add remaining ¼ cup sugar, 1 tablespoon at a time, beating until stiff, glossy peaks form. Fold beaten whites into batter just until whites are no longer visible. Scrape batter into prepared pan and spread evenly.

5 Bake until toothpick inserted into center of cake comes out clean, about 1 hour. Let cool completely in pan on wire rack. Run thin knife around edge of cake to loosen from side and center tube of pan. Remove cake from pan and wrap in foil. Refrigerate at least 1 day or up to 5 days before serving.

1½ cups walnuts, chopped

1 cup dried figs, chopped

1 cup dried currants

1½ cups all-purpose flour

1 teaspoon baking powder

½ teaspoon ground cinnamon

¼ teaspoon ground nutmeg

½ cup (1 stick) unsalted butter, softened

1 cup sugar

▲ 3 large eggs, separated and at room temperature

2 teaspoons vanilla extract

½ cup dark rum

½ teaspoon salt

PER SERVING (1/24 of cake): 183 Cal, 9 g Total Fat, 3 g Sat Fat, 0 g Trans Fat, 37 mg Chol, 81 mg Sod, 22 g Carb, 13 g Sugar, 2 g Fib, 3 g Prot, 33 mg Calc.

CRANBERRY-PECAN
QUICK BREAD

CRANBERRY-PECAN QUICK BREAD

1 Preheat oven to 375°F. Spray 4½ x 8½-inch loaf pan with nonstick spray.

2 Whisk together all-purpose flour, white whole wheat flour, sugar, baking powder, baking soda, and salt in large bowl. Whisk together egg substitute, oil, and orange zest and juice in small bowl. Add egg mixture to flour mixture, stirring just until flour mixture is moistened. Stir in cranberries and pecans. Scrape batter into prepared pan and spread evenly.

3 Bake until loaf begins to pull away from sides of pan and toothpick inserted into center comes out clean, 50 55 minutes. Let cool in pan on wire rack 10 minutes. Remove loaf from pan and let cool completely on rack.

1 cup all-purpose flour

1 cup white whole wheat flour

¾ cup sugar

1½ teaspoons baking powder

½ teaspoon baking soda

⅓ teaspoon salt

▲ ½ cup fat-free egg substitute

¼ cup canola oil

2 teaspoons grated orange zest

¾ cup orange juice

▲ 1 cup coarsely chopped fresh or frozen cranberries

½ cup coarsely chopped pecans

PER SERVING (1⁄16 of loaf): 148 Cal, 6 g Total Fat, 1 g Sat Fat, 0 g Trans Fat, 0 mg Chol, 176 mg Sod, 22 g Carb, 8 g Sugar, 2 g Fib, 3 g Prot, 17 mg Calc.

★ **FYI** ★ To turn a slice of this tasty loaf into a healthy breakfast, serve it with fat-free cream cheese and fresh orange wedges (1 tablespoon of light cream cheese per serving will increase the **PointsPlus** value by **1**).

NEW YORK CHEESECAKE

PER SERVING

1 tablespoon unsalted butter, softened

¼ cup reduced-fat graham cracker crumbs

1½ (8-ounce) packages light cream cheese (Neufchâtel), softened

½ cup sugar

▲ 3 large egg whites

1½ tablespoons cornstarch

1½ teaspoons vanilla extract

1 cup reduced-fat sour cream

1 Preheat oven to 400°F. Grease bottom of 9-inch springform pan with butter. Add cracker crumbs, shaking and tilting pan to coat evenly. Refrigerate until chilled, about 15 minutes.

2 With electric mixer on medium speed, beat cream cheese and sugar in large bowl until light and fluffy, about 3 minutes. Beat in egg whites, cornstarch, and vanilla. Reduce mixer speed to low; beat in sour cream just until blended.

3 Pour batter into prepared pan. Bake until cheesecake is almost set in center, 35–40 minutes. Turn off oven and prop open door with wooden spoon. Let cheesecake cool in oven 30 minutes. Let cool completely in pan on wire rack. Refrigerate at least 3 hours before serving.

PER SERVING (¹⁄₁₂ of cake): 108 Cal, 8 g Total Fat, 5 g Sat Fat, 0 g Trans Fat, 24 mg Chol, 102 mg Sod, 4 g Carb, 1 g Sugar, 0 g Fib, 4 g Prot, 53 mg Calc.

★ **FYI** ★ Top the cheesecake with a mix of sliced strawberries, raspberries, blackberries, and blueberries.

194   BEST DARN FOOD EVER!

ORANGE-AND-ROSEMARY-SCENTED STRAWBERRY SHORTCAKE

6 PointsPlus® value

PER SERVING

SERVES 12

1 Preheat oven to 400°F. Spray 9-inch round baking pan with nonstick spray.

2 To make shortcake, whisk together flour, granulated sugar, baking powder, salt, and baking soda in large bowl. Stir together buttermilk, oil, egg, orange zest, and rosemary in medium bowl. Add buttermilk mixture to flour mixture, stirring just until flour mixture is moistened. Scrape batter into prepared pan and spread evenly.

3 Bake until top of shortcake is golden brown and toothpick inserted into center comes out clean, about 20 minutes. Let cool in pan on wire rack 5 minutes. Remove shortcake from pan and let cool completely on rack.

4 To make filling, with potato masher, crush ½ cup of strawberries with granulated sugar in large bowl. Add remaining strawberries and stir until combined.

5 With long serrated knife, split shortcake in half. Place bottom of shortcake on serving plate. Fold together whipped topping and sour cream in medium bowl until just combined; spoon over bottom of shortcake. Top with about two-thirds of strawberry mixture; cover with top of shortcake. Dust with confectioners' sugar. Serve remaining strawberry mixture alongside.

SHORTCAKE

2 cups all-purpose flour

½ cup granulated sugar

2 teaspoons baking powder

½ teaspoon salt

½ teaspoon baking soda

¾ cup low-fat buttermilk

¼ cup canola oil

▲ 1 large egg

2 teaspoons grated orange zest

½ teaspoon minced fresh rosemary

FILLING AND TOPPING

▲ 6 cups fresh strawberries, hulled and thickly sliced

¼ cup granulated sugar

1½ cups thawed frozen fat-free whipped topping

▲ 1 cup fat-free sour cream

1 tablespoon confectioners' sugar

PER SERVING (1/12 of shortcake): 222 Cal, 6 g Total Fat, 1 g Sat Fat, 0 g Trans Fat, 21 mg Chol, 299 mg Sod, 30 g Carb, 16 g Sugar, 2 g Fib, 4 g Prot, 80 mg Calc.

★ **FYI** ★ The addition of orange zest and fresh rosemary is what makes this recipe special. If you are a traditionalist, you can leave them out.

BAKED PUMPKIN CUSTARDS WITH SUGARED WALNUTS

SERVES 12

PER SERVING

SUGARED WALNUTS

⅓ cup granulated sugar

2 tablespoons water

¾ cup + 2 tablespoons walnuts, coarsely chopped

CUSTARD

2 cups low-fat (1%) milk

¾ teaspoon ground cinnamon

¼ teaspoon ground nutmeg

¼ teaspoon ground allspice

Pinch ground cloves

½ cup packed light brown sugar

▲ 4 large eggs

▲ 2 large egg whites

▲ ⅔ cup canned pumpkin puree (not pumpkin pie mix)

2 teaspoons vanilla extract

1 Preheat oven to 350°F. Place 12 (4-ounce) custard cups in large roasting pan.

2 To make sugared walnuts, combine granulated sugar and water in small saucepan and bring to boil. Cook, swirling pan occasionally, until sugar turns deep caramel color, about 5 minutes (do not stir). Stir in ¾ cup of walnuts, tossing to coat. Quickly pour onto nonstick baking sheet; let cool completely. Break nut mixture into small pieces. Divide evenly among custard cups.

3 To make custard, combine milk, cinnamon, nutmeg, allspice, and cloves in medium saucepan and bring to simmer. Cook, stirring occasionally, 2 minutes.

4 Meanwhile, whisk together brown sugar, eggs, and egg whites in large bowl. Gradually whisk about ½ cup of hot milk mixture into egg mixture to temper it. Whisk in remaining milk mixture until smooth. Whisk in pumpkin and vanilla until blended. Divide evenly among custard cups.

5 Place roasting pan in oven; add enough boiling water to pan to come halfway up sides of custard cups. Bake until tip of small knife inserted into center of custard comes out clean, 20–30 minutes. Transfer custards to wire rack and let cool completely. Refrigerate at least 4 hours or up to overnight. Sprinkle evenly with remaining 2 tablespoons walnuts before serving.

PER SERVING (1 custard): 147 Cal, 7 g Total Fat, 1 g Sat Fat, 0 g Trans Fat, 74 mg Chol, 52 mg Sod, 18 g Carb, 16 g Sugar, 1 g Fib, 5 g Prot, 76 mg Calc.

ALL AMERICAN

The word *pumpkin* comes from "pepon," the Greek word for large melon. The French changed the word to pompon, the English changed it to pumpion, and the American colonists changed it to pumpkin. Native Americans roasted strips of pumpkin over a fire. The colonists cleverly sliced off the top of a whole pumpkin, removed the seeds, and filled the hollow with milk, spices, and honey before baking it in hot ashes.

BAKED PUMPKIN CUSTARDS WITH
SUGARED WALNUTS

INDIAN PUDDING

PER SERVING

4 cups reduced-fat (2%) milk

¾ cup yellow cornmeal

½ cup light (mild) molasses

⅓ cup sugar

2 tablespoons unsalted butter, cut into pieces

▲ 1 large egg, lightly beaten

¾ teaspoon ground cinnamon

½ teaspoon ground ginger

½ teaspoon salt

¼ teaspoon ground nutmeg

1½ pints vanilla fat-free frozen yogurt

1 Preheat oven to 300°F. Spray 2-quart round or square baking dish with nonstick spray.

2 Gently heat 3 cups of milk in medium saucepan until it begins to steam. Slowly stir in cornmeal and cook, stirring constantly, until thickened, about 5 minutes; remove saucepan from heat.

3 Stir together molasses, sugar, butter, egg, cinnamon, ginger, salt, and nutmeg in medium bowl until butter is melted. Add molasses mixture to cornmeal mixture, stirring until blended well. Pour into prepared baking dish.

4 Set baking dish in large roasting pan and put in oven. Add enough boiling water to roasting pan to come halfway up side of baking dish. Bake 30 minutes. Carefully pour remaining 1 cup milk over pudding.

5 Bake until pudding is set, about 1 hour 45 minutes. Let cool slightly. Spoon pudding evenly into 12 dessert dishes or bowls. Top each serving with ¼-cup scoop of frozen yogurt.

PER SERVING (¹⁄₁₂ of pudding and ¼ cup frozen yogurt): 231 Cal, 4 g Total Fat, 2 g Sat Fat, 0 g Trans Fat, 37 mg Chol, 187 mg Sod, 41 g Carb, 31 g Sugar, 0 g Fib, 7 g Prot, 216 mg Calc.

ALL AMERICAN

Cornmeal and molasses were staples in the American colonies, so it didn't take long for the settlers to find creative ways to use these ingredients in everyday cooking. Molasses, less expensive than sugar, was the sweetener of choice in many desserts. This pudding's name is a nod to the term "Indian," which means Indian meal or cornmeal.

TAPIOCA PUDDING WITH SPICED CHERRY AND APRICOT COMPOTE

1 To make fruit compote, combine water, ⅓ cup of sugar, the apricots, cherries, lemon, cinnamon stick, and bay leaf in medium saucepan; bring to boil. Reduce heat and simmer, covered, until fruit is softened and liquid is syrupy, about 10 minutes. Remove saucepan from heat and let cool. Remove cinnamon stick and bay leaf and discard.

2 To make pudding, combine remaining ⅓ cup sugar, the milk, egg substitute, and tapioca in medium saucepan; let stand 5 minutes. Bring to boil over medium heat. Cook, stirring constantly, 5 minutes. Remove saucepan from heat and let pudding cool to room temperature.

3 Divide pudding evenly among 6 dessert dishes. Top evenly with fruit compote.

1½ cups water

⅔ cup sugar

¾ cup dried apricots, preferably California, cut into strips

¼ cup dried tart cherries

½ lemon, thinly sliced

½ (3-inch) cinnamon stick

1 bay leaf

▲ 2 ½ cups fat-free milk

▲ ½ cup fat-free egg substitute

¼ cup quick-cooking tapioca

PER SERVING (1 dessert): 180 Cal, 0 g Total Fat, 0 g Sat Fat, 0 g Trans Fat, 2 mg Chol, 77 mg Sod, 43 g Carb, 32 g Sugar, 3 g Fib, 6 g Prot, 153 mg Calc.

★ **FYI** ★ Other dried fruits can be used in this compote: substitute dried blueberries or cranberries for the dried cherries, or use pears instead of apricots.

EASY PEACH MELBA

EASY PEACH MELBA

SERVES 4

1 Press raspberries through sieve set over small saucepan; discard seeds. Stir in jam, sugar, lime juice, and cornstarch. Cook over medium-low heat, stirring, until sauce bubbles and thickens, about 3 minutes. Transfer raspberry mixture to small bowl; refrigerate until cool, about 45 minutes.

2 To serve, divide peach wedges among 4 dessert dishes or goblets. Drizzle each serving with 2 tablespoons of raspberry sauce. Top each dessert with ⅓-cup scoop of frozen yogurt; top evenly with remaining sauce. Serve immediately.

▲ 2 ½ cups fresh raspberries (about two 6-ounce containers)

¼ cup seedless raspberry jam

2 tablespoons sugar

2 teaspoons lime juice

1½ teaspoons cornstarch

▲ 4 peaches, pitted and cut into wedges

1⅓ cups vanilla fat-free frozen yogurt

PER SERVING (1 dessert): 258 Cal, 1 g Total Fat, 0 g Sat Fat, 0 g Trans Fat, 11 mg Chol, 66 mg Sod, 58 g Carb, 38 g Sugar, 7 g Fib, 6 g Prot, 128 mg Calc.

ALL AMERICAN

At the turn of the 20th century, legendary chef Auguste Escoffier created the dessert peach melba in honor of famed opera singer Nellie Melba. Although the dessert was first served in London, it quickly became all the rage in America.

LEMON-LIME SHERBET

3
PointsPlus®
value

PER SERVING

¾ cup superfine sugar

¾ cup ice water

½ cup lime juice

Grated zest of ½ lemon

▲ ¼ cup pasteurized liquid egg whites

1 Stir together sugar and ice water in medium bowl until sugar is dissolved. Stir in lime juice and lemon zest. Pour lime mixture into ice-cream maker and freeze according to manufacturer's instructions until partially frozen. (Or pour lime mixture into shallow metal pan and freeze, stirring occasionally, until partially frozen.)

2 With electric mixer on medium speed, beat egg whites in medium bowl until stiff peaks form when beaters are lifted. Transfer lime mixture to large bowl. Fold in one-third of beaten egg whites to lighten mixture, then fold in remaining egg whites until no longer visible. Spoon lime mixture back into ice-cream maker and freeze until firm. (Or return mixture to baking pan and freeze, stirring occasionally, until firm, about 2 hours.)

3 Transfer sherbet to freezer container and freeze until firm, at least 2 hours or up to 6 hours.

PER SERVING (¼ of sherbet): 106 Cal, 0 g Total Fat, 0 g Sat Fat, 0 g Trans Fat, 0 mg Chol, 28 mg Sod, 30 g Carb, 28 g Sugar, 0 g Fib, 2 g Prot, 9 mg Calc.

★ **FYI** ★ The addition of milk or beaten egg whites turns sorbet into sherbet. In our recipe, the beaten egg whites give the sherbet a lighter texture. Refrigerated pasteurized liquid egg whites are heated, which ensures that they do not contain salmonella and are safe to consume uncooked.

RHUBARB-RASPBERRY OATMEAL BARS

PointsPlus® value

PER SERVING

1 Preheat oven to 375°F.

2 To make filling, toss together rhubarb, raspberries, orange zest, and ⅓ cup of brown sugar in 2½-quart baking dish. Bake until rhubarb is tender, about 35 minutes. Let cool.

3 Reduce oven temperature to 350°F. Spray 8-inch square baking pan with nonstick spray.

4 To make dough/topping, stir together flour, oats, remaining ⅓ cup brown sugar, the egg white, and salt in medium bowl. With your fingers, rub in butter until mixture resembles coarse crumbs.

5 Pat generous half of oat mixture into bottom of prepared baking pan. Stir hazelnuts into remaining oat mixture. Spoon rhubarb mixture evenly over oat mixture; sprinkle evenly with oat-hazelnut mixture.

6 Bake until topping is firm and lightly golden, about 45 minutes. Let cool completely in pan on wire rack. Cut bars lengthwise into 4 strips, then cut each strip across into 3 pieces.

▲ 1½ pounds rhubarb, cut into ½-inch pieces

▲ 1 (6-ounce) container fresh raspberries

Grated zest of ½ orange

⅔ cup packed light brown sugar

¾ cup all-purpose flour

¾ cup rolled (old-fashioned) oats

▲ 1 large egg white, lightly beaten

¼ teaspoon salt

3 tablespoons unsalted butter, cut into pieces

⅓ cup hazelnuts, toasted and chopped

PER SERVING (1 bar cookie): 164 Cal, 6 g Total Fat, 2 g Sat Fat, 0 g Trans Fat, 8 mg Chol, 59 mg Sod, 26 g Carb, 14 g Sugar, 3 g Fib, 3 g Prot, 71 mg Calc.

MORAVIAN SPICE COOKIES

MORAVIAN SPICE COOKIES

MAKES ABOUT 6 ½ DOZEN

1 Whisk together flour, ginger, cinnamon, mustard powder, baking soda, allspice, and cloves in small bowl.

2 With electric mixer on medium speed, beat butter and brown sugar in large bowl until light and fluffy, about 3 minutes. Add molasses and beat until blended well. Reduce mixer speed to low; add half of flour mixture, beating just until blended. Beat in remaining flour mixture until stiff dough is formed. Divide dough into 4 equal portions. Wrap each portion in plastic wrap; refrigerate at least 4 hours or up to overnight.

3 Place racks in upper and lower thirds of oven and preheat oven to 350°F.

4 On lightly floured work surface with floured rolling pin, roll out one piece of dough to ¹⁄₁₆-inch thickness. With floured 2½-inch fluted round cutter, cut out cookies. Place ½ inch apart on ungreased large baking sheets.

5 Bake until cookies are set but not browned, 6–8 minutes, rotating baking sheets halfway through baking time. Let cool on baking sheets 1 minute, then with pancake spatula transfer cookies to wire racks to cool completely. Repeat with remaining dough, gathering and rerolling scraps, making total of 78 cookies.

1½ cups all-purpose flour

1 teaspoon ground ginger

¾ teaspoon ground cinnamon

½ teaspoon mustard powder

½ teaspoon baking soda

¼ teaspoon ground allspice

¼ teaspoon ground cloves

4 tablespoons unsalted butter, at room temperature

⅓ cup packed brown sugar

½ cup light (mild) molasses

PER SERVING (3 cookies): 72 Cal, 2 g Total Fat, 1 g Sat Fat, 0 g Trans Fat, 5 mg Chol, 29 mg Sod, 13 g Carb, 7 g Sugar, 0 g Fib, 1 g Prot, 24 mg Calc.

ALL AMERICAN

In 1752 a sect of Protestants traveled from Moravia in Eastern Europe to Winston-Salem, North Carolina seeking religious freedom. Among the many recipes they brought with them were ones for paper-thin molasses-and-spice-laden cookies. Stored in an airtight container, they will keep up to 2 months.

CHOCOLATY

HOT FUDGE SAUCE, PAGE 225

★ CAKES ★

Chocolate Angel Food Cake with Warm Chocolate Drizzle, 209

Bittersweet Chocolate and Almond Cake, 210

Streusel-Topped Chocolate Chip Coffee Cake, 212

Double-Ginger Chocolate Gingerbread, 213

Devil's Food Cupcakes with White Icing Squiggles, 215

★ PUDDING DESSERTS ★

Mexican-Style Chocolate Pudding, 216

Warm Chocolate Pudding Cake with Frozen Yogurt, 217

Black Bottom Pudding Pie, 218

★ COOKIES ★

Whoopie Pies, 221

Pecan Fudge Brownies, 222

★ MORE ★

Cocoa-Dusted Bittersweet Chocolate Truffles, 224

Hot Fudge Sauce, 225

CHOCOLATE ANGEL FOOD CAKE WITH WARM CHOCOLATE DRIZZLE

6 PointsPlus© value

PER SERVING

1 Place oven rack in lower third of oven and preheat oven to 375°F.

2 Sift flour, cocoa, and salt into medium bowl. With electric mixer on medium speed, beat egg whites and cream of tartar in large bowl until soft peaks form when beaters are lifted. Add sugar, 2 tablespoons at a time, beating until stiff, glossy peaks form when beaters are lifted. Beat in vanilla.

3 Sift cocoa mixture, one-third at a time, over beaten egg whites, gently folding it in with rubber spatula just until cocoa is no longer visible. (Be careful not to overmix.)

4 Scrape batter into ungreased 10-inch tube pan; spread evenly. Bake until cake springs back when lightly pressed, 35–40 minutes. Invert pan onto its legs or neck of bottle and let cool completely.

5 Run thin knife around edge of cake to loosen it from side and center tube of pan. Remove cake from pan and put on serving plate.

6 To make chocolate glaze, put chocolate in small microwavable bowl. Microwave on High 30 seconds; stir. Microwave another 15 seconds; stir. Continue to microwave until chocolate is melted, about 15 seconds longer. Cut cake into 12 wedges and place on plates. Drizzle glaze over each slice of cake.

1½ cups cake flour

½ cup unsweetened cocoa

½ teaspoon salt

12 large egg whites, at room temperature

1 teaspoon cream of tartar

1½ cups sugar

2 teaspoons vanilla extract

4 ounces semisweet chocolate, chopped

PER SERVING (¹⁄₁₂ of cake and 2 teaspoons glaze): 200 Cal, 4 g Total Fat, 2 g Sat Fat, 0 g Trans Fat, 0 mg Chol, 153 mg Sod, 41 g Carb, 24 g Sugar, 3 g Fib, 7 g Prot, 12 mg Calc.

★ **FYI** ★ The key to beating the egg whites just enough is to beat them just until they form stiff, glossy peaks. If you are unsure of exactly how much to beat them, keep in mind that it is better to slightly under beat them. When overbeaten, egg whites resemble bits of cotton and they separate and leak liquid. If that happens, toss them out and begin again.

BITTERSWEET CHOCOLATE AND ALMOND CAKE

SERVES 24

4 PointsPlus® value

PER SERVING

2 cups all-purpose flour

1 cup sugar

2 teaspoons baking powder

½ teaspoon baking soda

½ teaspoon salt

⅔ cup unsweetened cocoa

½ cup boiling water

1 cup low-fat buttermilk

⅓ cup canola oil

▲ 1 large egg

▲ 1 large egg white

1 teaspoon almond extract

⅔ cup bittersweet chocolate chips

⅓ cup whole blanched almonds, finely chopped

2 tablespoons confectioners' sugar

1 Preheat oven to 350°F. Spray 10-inch Bundt pan with nonstick spray.

2 Whisk together flour, sugar, baking powder, baking soda, and salt in medium bowl. Put cocoa in small bowl and pour boiling water over; whisk until smooth. Whisk together buttermilk, oil, egg, egg white, and almond extract in large bowl; stir in cocoa mixture until blended. Gradually add flour mixture, stirring just until mixed well. Stir in chocolate chips and almonds.

3 Pour batter into prepared pan. Bake until toothpick inserted into center of cake comes out clean, 40–45 minutes. Let cool in pan on wire rack 10 minutes. Remove cake from pan and let cool completely on rack. Dust with confectioners' sugar.

PER SERVING (¹⁄₂₄ of cake): 144 Cal, 8 g Total Fat, 2 g Sat Fat, 0 g Trans Fat, 9 mg Chol, 137 mg Sod, 20 g Carb, 9 g Sugar, 2 g Fib, 3 g Prot, 32 mg Calc.

★ **FYI** ★ Bittersweet chocolate chips can be found in supermarkets in the baking aisle and in specialty food stores.

BITTERSWEET CHOCOLATE
AND ALMOND CAKE

STREUSEL-TOPPED CHOCOLATE CHIP COFFEE CAKE

SERVES 24

PER SERVING

STREUSEL

½ cup packed brown sugar

2 tablespoons unsweetened cocoa

2 teaspoons canola oil

⅓ cup walnuts, finely chopped

CAKE

2 ¼ cups whole wheat pastry flour

¾ cup granulated sugar

1½ teaspoons baking powder

½ teaspoon baking soda

½ teaspoon salt

1 cup plain low-fat yogurt

▲ 2 large eggs

¼ cup canola oil

2 teaspoons vanilla extract

½ cup mini semisweet chocolate chips

1 Preheat oven to 350°F. Spray 9 x 13-inch baking pan with nonstick spray.

2 To make streusel, with your fingers, rub together brown sugar, cocoa, and oil in small bowl until blended well. Stir in walnuts.

3 To make cake, whisk together pastry flour, granulated sugar, baking powder, baking soda, and salt in large bowl. Whisk together yogurt, eggs, oil, and vanilla in medium bowl. Add yogurt mixture to flour mixture, stirring just until flour mixture is moistened. Stir in chocolate chips.

4 Scrape batter into prepared pan and spread evenly; sprinkle with streusel. Bake until toothpick inserted into center of cake comes out clean, about 25 minutes. Let cool in pan on wire rack at least 30 minutes.

PER SERVING (1/24 of cake): 131 Cal, 5 g Total Fat, 1 g Sat Fat, 0 g Trans Fat, 19 mg Chol, 123 mg Sod, 19 g Carb, 12 g Sugar, 2 g Fib, 3 g Prot, 39 mg Calc.

DOUBLE-GINGER
CHOCOLATE GINGERBREAD

4
PointsPlus®
value

PER SERVING

1 Preheat oven to 350°F. Spray 8-inch square baking pan with nonstick spray.

2 Whisk together flour, ground ginger, cinnamon, baking soda, and salt in large bowl. Stir in chocolate chips and crystallized ginger. Whisk together molasses, boiling water, brown sugar, and cocoa in medium bowl until blended. Whisk in oil and egg. Add molasses mixture to flour mixture, stirring until blended well.

3 Pour batter into prepared pan. Bake until toothpick inserted into center of cake comes out clean, 30–35 minutes. Let cake cool in pan on wire rack 15 minutes. Remove cake from pan and let cool completely on rack.

PER SERVING (1/16 of cake): 162 Cal, 6 g Total Fat, 2 g Sat Fat, 0 g Trans Fat, 13 mg Chol, 127 mg Sod, 26 g Carb, 13 g Sugar, 1 g Fib, 2 g Prot, 49 mg Calc.

1¾ cups all-purpose flour

2½ teaspoons ground ginger

1 teaspoon ground cinnamon

1 teaspoon baking soda

¼ teaspoon salt

½ cup bittersweet chocolate chips

¼ cup finely chopped crystallized ginger

⅔ cup light (mild) molasses

⅔ cup boiling water

⅔ cup packed light brown sugar

¼ cup unsweetened cocoa

¼ cup canola oil

▲ 1 large egg

DEVIL'S FOOD CUPCAKES WITH WHITE ICING SQUIGGLES

DEVIL'S FOOD CUPCAKES WITH
WHITE ICING SQUIGGLES

6 PointsPlus® value

PER SERVING

1 Preheat oven to 375°F. Spray 12-cup muffin pan with nonstick spray.

2 To make cupcakes, whisk together flour, sugar, cocoa, grated chocolate, espresso powder, baking powder, salt, and baking soda in medium bowl. Whisk together egg, egg white, milk, sour cream, oil, and vanilla in small bowl. Add milk mixture to flour mixture, stirring just until blended.

3 Fill prepared muffin cups about two-thirds full with batter. Bake until toothpick inserted into center of cupcake comes out clean, about 25 minutes. Let cool in pan on wire rack 10 minutes. Remove cupcakes from pan and let cool completely on rack.

4 To make glaze, place chocolate chips and milk in small microwavable bowl. Microwave on High 30 seconds; stir. Microwave until chocolate is melted and mixture is smooth, 10–15 seconds longer. Let stand 10 minutes to cool and thicken slightly.

5 Dip tops of cupcakes into glaze, turning to coat. Let cupcakes cool on rack until glaze is set, about 20 minutes. Pipe little circles of icing in line across tops of cupcakes.

PER SERVING (1 cupcake): 203 Cal, 9 g Total Fat, 3 g Sat Fat, 0 g Trans Fat, 19 mg Chol, 202 mg Sod, 30 g Carb, 17 g Sugar, 2 g Fib, 4 g Prot, 49 mg Calc.

CUPCAKES

1 cup cake flour

¾ cup sugar

½ cup unsweetened cocoa

1 ounce semisweet chocolate, grated

2 teaspoons instant espresso powder

1 teaspoon baking powder

½ teaspoon salt

¼ teaspoon baking soda

▲ 1 large egg

▲ 1 egg white

▲ ½ cup fat-free milk

▲ ½ cup fat-free sour cream

¼ cup canola oil

1 teaspoon vanilla extract

GLAZE

½ cup dark or semisweet chocolate chips

▲ ¼ cup fat-free milk

White decorating Icing

ALL AMERICAN

These very chocolaty cupcakes are a nod to the classic Hostess cupcakes. They were first created in 1919, but it wasn't until 1950 when its signature vanilla crème filling and seven-squiggle decoration were added that sales really took off.

MEXICAN-STYLE CHOCOLATE PUDDING

SERVES 6   20 MIN

PER SERVING

2 ounces Mexican semisweet chocolate, chopped

½ cup packed brown sugar

⅓ cup unsweetened cocoa

3 tablespoons cornstarch

Pinch salt

2 ½ cups fat-free chocolate milk

2 teaspoons vanilla extract

1 Combine chocolate, brown sugar, cocoa, cornstarch, and salt in medium saucepan. Whisk in 1 cup of chocolate milk and cook over medium heat, whisking, until chocolate is melted and mixture is smooth.

2 Gradually whisk in remaining 1½ cups chocolate milk and cook, stirring constantly, until large bubbles pop on surface and pudding is thickened and smooth, about 6 minutes. Remove saucepan from heat and stir in vanilla.

3 Divide pudding evenly among 6 dessert dishes or custard cups. Serve warm or refrigerate to serve chilled, pressing piece of plastic wrap directly onto surface of each pudding to prevent skin from forming, if desired.

PER SERVING (½ cup): 209 Cal, 4 g Total Fat, 2 g Sat Fat, 0 g Trans Fat, 2 mg Chol, 91 mg Sod, 43 g Carb, 35 g Sugar, 2 g Fib, 5 g Prot, 135 mg Calc.

★ **FYI** ★ Unlike other types of chocolate, Mexican chocolate is laced with cinnamon and coated with coarse sugar. The best-known brand is Ibarra, which packs the chocolate in a distinctive yellow and red hexagon-shaped box. It is available in specialty food stores and online.

WARM CHOCOLATE PUDDING CAKE WITH FROZEN YOGURT

5 PointsPlus® value PER SERVING

SERVES 9

- ¾ cup all-purpose flour
- ¾ cup granulated sugar
- ⅓ + ¼ cup unsweetened cocoa
- 2 teaspoons baking powder
- ¼ teaspoon baking soda
- ¼ teaspoon salt
- ½ cup low-fat (1%) milk
- 1 tablespoon unsalted butter, melted
- 2 teaspoons vanilla extract
- ⅓ cup packed brown sugar
- 1⅔ cups boiling water
- 1½ pints vanilla fat-free frozen yogurt

1 Preheat oven to 350°F. Spray 9-inch square baking pan or baking dish with nonstick spray.

2 Whisk together flour, granulated sugar, ⅓ cup of cocoa, the baking powder, baking soda, and salt in large bowl. Make a well in center of flour mixture; combine milk, butter, and vanilla in well; stir just until it forms smooth batter; pour into prepared pan.

3 Stir together brown sugar and remaining ¼ cup cocoa in small bowl. Sprinkle evenly over batter. Slowly pour boiling water over batter in zigzag fashion (do not stir).

4 Bake until top of pudding is set, about 35 minutes. Let cool in pan on wire rack at least 30 minutes. Cut into 9 squares and divide among 9 dessert dishes. Place ⅓-cup scoop of frozen yogurt alongside each serving.

PER SERVING (1 dessert): 188 Cal, 2 g Total Fat, 1 g Sat Fat, 0 g Trans Fat, 8 mg Chol, 259 mg Sod, 41 g Carb, 28 g Sugar, 2 g Fib, 4 g Prot, 99 mg Calc.

ALL AMERICAN

In her 1824 book *The Virginia Housewife,* Mary Randolf praises pudding cakes for their forgiving nature. She tells her readers that these desserts are far easier to prepare than cakes and whether they are baked a little more or a little less doesn't matter. In New England, chocolate pudding cake is called chocolate sponge, while in Maryland it's called chocolate cake-top pudding.

BLACK BOTTOM PUDDING PIE

5
PointsPlus©
value

PER SERVING

¼ cup sugar

3 tablespoons all-purpose flour

Pinch salt

1½ cups low-fat (1%) milk

▲ 1 large egg

1 tablespoon coconut-flavored rum or 1 teaspoon rum extract

¼ cup dark chocolate chips

1 (6-ounce) prepared reduced-fat graham cracker crust

1¼ cups thawed frozen fat-free whipped topping

½ ounce semisweet chocolate, grated

1 Whisk together sugar, flour, and salt in medium saucepan. Whisk in milk and egg until blended; set over medium heat. Cook, stirring constantly, until custard is thickened, coats back of spoon, and begins to bubble, about 4 minutes. Let bubble 1 minute, stirring. Remove saucepan from heat.

2 Press half of custard through sieve set over medium bowl. Stir in rum. Refrigerate until well chilled, about 30 minutes.

3 Meanwhile, add chocolate chips to hot custard in saucepan, stirring until chocolate is melted and mixture is smooth. Press through same sieve over crust, spread chocolate evenly. Refrigerate until custard is set, about 30 minutes.

4 Fold ¼ cup of whipped topping into chilled vanilla custard. Spread evenly over chocolate custard. Spread remaining 1 cup whipped topping over top of pie. Refrigerate pie at least 3 hours or up to overnight. Just before serving, sprinkle with grated chocolate.

PER SERVING (⅛ of pie): 200 Cal, 6 g Total Fat, 2 g Sat Fat, 2 g Trans Fat, 29 mg Chol, 156 mg Sod, 32 g Carb, 17 g Sugar, 0 g Fib, 4 g Prot, 59 mg Calc.

★ **FYI** ★ According to James Beard in his book *American Cookery,* black bottom pie began appearing in cookbooks around the turn of the 20th century. It didn't really catch on, however, until Duncan Hines made note of it in one of his popular cookbooks of the day.

BLACK BOTTOM PUDDING PIE

DRESS IT UP WITH CHOCOLATE!

There are several ways to turn simple desserts into WOW desserts. Garnishes such as chocolate leaves, curls, and shavings are easy to prepare—and a lot of fun too.

★ TRY THIS! ★

• **Grated chocolate** This super simple garnish can dress up chocolate cakes or pies with ease. Using the large or small holes of a box grater or Microplane grater, grate white, milk, or semisweet chocolate onto a sheet of wax paper and use the gratings to cover the edge of a dessert, the center, or the entire top.

• **Short chocolate curls** Small and delicate, these curls are ideal for piling onto chocolate pudding, sorbet, or mousse. Using a large bar or piece of room temperature dark, milk, or white chocolate, peel curls from the bar with a vegetable peeler, allowing the curls to fall onto a sheet of wax paper. Refrigerate until ready to serve.

• **Chocolate shavings** Make these the same way as short chocolate curls but use very short, quick strokes to create slightly curled shavings. These dress up just about any chocolate treat—even ice cream sodas or fruit smoothies.

• **Long chocolate curls** Slim and elegant, these curls are also called cigarettes. With a long, narrow spatula, spread melted semisweet or bittersweet chocolate over the back of a baking sheet or jelly-roll pan until slightly less than ¼ inch thick. Let the chocolate stand at room temperature until set. Holding a wide spatula at a 45-degree angle on top of the chocolate, push the spatula away from you, shaving off long, narrow curls. Use a bamboo skewer to transfer them to a wax paper–lined plate and refrigerate until ready to use.

• **Chocolate cut-outs** Line a baking sheet with a sheet of wax paper. Use a narrow metal spatula to spread an ⅛-inch-thick layer of melted chocolate; let the chocolate stand until almost set. Using small cookie cutters, cut out shapes, leaving them on the baking sheet. Refrigerate until the chocolate is hard, then remove the shapes from the wax paper.

• **Chocolate leaves** Wash and thoroughly dry nontoxic leaves such as rose or lemon. Brush the bottom (veiny side) of each leaf with a thick layer of melted semisweet, milk, or white chocolate and place each leaf, chocolate-side up, on a wax paper–lined flat plate or jelly-roll pan. Refrigerate until the chocolate is set. Gently peel off each leaf and return the chocolate leaves, vein-side up to the plate and refrigerate until ready to use.

★ TYPES OF CHOCOLATE ★

• **Semisweet chocolate** is a great all-purpose chocolate with a mild, sweet flavor. It is usually interchangeable with bittersweet chocolate in recipes.

• **Bittersweet Chocolate** is less sweet than semisweet chocolate. The percentage of chocolate liquor it contains is listed on its package and ranges from 60 to 80 percent. The higher the percentage, the more intense and bittersweet the flavor.

• **Milk Chocolate** contains dried milk powder and more sugar than semisweet chocolate. It melts at a lower temperature than other chocolates, as it is sensitive to heat.

• **White Chocolate** is not chocolate at all, as it doesn't contain chocolate liquor. It is made of cocoa butter, sugar, and vanilla flavor.

WHOOPIE PIES

1 Place oven racks in upper and lower thirds of oven and preheat oven to 425°F.

2 Whisk together flour, cocoa, baking soda, and salt in small bowl.

3 With electric mixer on medium speed, beat sugar, butter, oil, and egg white in medium bowl until light and fluffy. Reduce mixer speed to low. Beat in flour mixture just until blended then stir in milk just until blended. Drop batter by spoonfuls onto large ungreased baking sheets, making total of 36 cookies.

4 Bake until tops of cookies spring back when lightly pressed, 5–7 minutes. Let cool completely on baking sheets on wire racks.

5 Spoon 2 teaspoons marshmallow crème on bottoms of 18 cookies. Cover with remaining cookies.

PER SERVING (1 cookie): 188 Cal, 7 g Total Fat, 2 g Sat Fat, 0 g Trans Fat, 8 mg Chol, 252 mg Sod, 31 g Carb, 16 g Sugar, 1 g Fib, 3 g Prot, 25 mg Calc.

1 cup all-purpose flour

¼ cup unsweetened cocoa

1 teaspoon baking soda

¼ teaspoon salt

½ cup sugar

2 tablespoons unsalted butter, at room temperature

2 tablespoons canola oil

1 large egg white

½ cup low-fat (1%) milk

¾ cup marshmallow crème

PECAN FUDGE BROWNIES

PER SERVING

½ cup all-purpose flour

¼ cup white whole wheat flour

½ teaspoon baking powder

¼ teaspoon salt

½ cup unsweetened cocoa

3 tablespoons unsalted butter, melted

1 cup sugar

▲ 1 large egg

▲ 2 large egg whites

2 teaspoons vanilla extract

¾ cup pecans, toasted and chopped

1 Preheat oven to 350°F. Line 8-inch square baking pan with foil, allowing foil to extend over rim of pan by 2 inches. Spray with nonstick spray.

2 Whisk together all-purpose flour, white whole wheat flour, baking powder, and salt in small bowl. Whisk together cocoa and butter in large bowl. Add sugar, egg, and egg whites to cocoa mixture, whisking until blended. Whisk in vanilla. Stir in flour mixture until blended. Stir in pecans.

3 Scrape batter into prepared pan and spread evenly. Bake until toothpick inserted into center of brownies comes out with moist crumbs clinging, 20–25 minutes. Let cool completely in pan on wire rack. Lift brownies from pan using foil as handles. Cut lengthwise into 4 strips, then cut each strip across into 4 squares.

PER SERVING (1 brownie): 120 Cal, 7 g Total Fat, 2 g Sat Fat, 0 g Trans Fat, 19 mg Chol, 66 mg Sod, 16 g Carb, 9 g Sugar, 2 g Fib, 3 g Prot, 14 mg Calc.

PECAN FUDGE BROWNIES AND
WHOOPIE PIES, PAGE 221

COCOA-DUSTED BITTERSWEET CHOCOLATE TRUFFLES

PER SERVING

8 ounces good-quality bittersweet chocolate, chopped

3 tablespoons unsalted butter

▲ ⅓ cup fat-free half-and-half

⅓ cup unsweetened cocoa powder

1 Combine chocolate and butter in medium heavy saucepan over low heat. Cook, stirring frequently, until melted and smooth; remove saucepan from heat. Stir in half-and-half until blended. Scrape chocolate mixture into medium bowl; let cool to room temperature. Cover bowl with plastic wrap; refrigerate until chocolate mixture is firm, at least 2 hours or up to 2 days.

2 Put cocoa in small bowl. Divide truffle mixture into 32 portions. Quickly roll each portion into ball, then roll in cocoa to coat evenly. Layer truffles between sheets of wax paper in covered container and refrigerate up to 1 week.

PER SERVING (1 truffle): 49 Cal, 4 g Total Fat, 2 g Sat Fat, 0 g Trans Fat, 3 mg Chol, 2 mg Sod, 4 g Carb, 3 g Sugar, 1 g Fib, 1 g Prot, 5 mg Calc.

★ **FYI** ★ If your prefer semisweet to bittersweet chocolate, by all means use it here.

HOT FUDGE SAUCE

20 MIN   **SERVES 24**   (makes 1½ cups)

1 Combine half-and-half and corn syrup in medium heavy saucepan over medium-high heat. Bring just to boil, whisking until smooth. Remove saucepan from heat; whisk in semisweet and bittersweet chocolates until melted and smooth.

2 Return chocolate mixture to boil. Cook, whisking constantly, 1 minute. Remove saucepan from heat and whisk in vanilla. Use or cool to room temperature. Transfer to covered container and refrigerate up to 1 month. Gently reheat before serving.

▲ 1 cup fat-free half-and-half

2 tablespoons light corn syrup

4 ounces semisweet chocolate, chopped

4 ounces bittersweet chocolate, chopped

2 teaspoons vanilla extract

PER SERVING (1 tablespoon): 60 Cal, 4 g Total Fat, 2 g Sat Fat, 0 g Trans Fat, 0 mg Chol, 10 mg Sod, 8 g Carb, 6 g Sugar, 1 g Fib, 1 g Prot, 14 mg Calc.

RECIPES BY *PointsPlus* VALUE

FISHERMAN'S WHARF CHOWDER, PAGE 147
AND BOSTON BROWN BREAD, PAGE 156

Philly Cheesesteak Sandwiches, 43

Slow-Cooker Chili Steak and Black Bean
  Tacos, 67

Smoky Pork BBQ on Buns, 78

Steak on Garlic Bread with Tomato-Avocado
  Salsa, 68

Turkey Tetrazzini, 23

PointsPlus value: **9**

Macaroni and Cheese, 52

Spicy Crab, Shrimp, and Cherry Tomato Gumbo, 80

Turkey, Spinach, and Mushroom Lasagna, 138

Weekend Spaghetti and Meatballs, 128

PointsPlus value: **10**

Beef Stew with Fire-Roasted Tomatoes
  and Bacon, 124

PointsPlus value: **11**

All Peppered Up Cajun Jambalaya, 71

Five-Way Cincinnati Turkey-Cayenne Chili, 77

Hearty Chicken with Parsley Dumplings, 135

Thyme-Crusted Turkey Pot Pie, 141

PointsPlus value: **12**

Cape Cod Clambake, 142

Succulent Pot Roast with Root Vegetables, 123

RECIPES THAT WORK WITH THE SIMPLY FILLING TECHNIQUE

CRUNCHY AND CRISPY
Main Dishes, Salads, Sides, and Breads
Steakhouse "Fries", 32
Red Flannel Hash, 33

CHEESY
Lunches & Sides
Wild Mushroom and Feta Cheese Frittata, 56

CREAMY
Light Bites, Soups, Chowders & Sides
Classic Deviled Eggs, 98
Little Havana–Style Black Bean Soup, 101
Autumn Squash, Apple, and Mushroom Soup, 103
Mashed Potatoes with Roasted Garlic, 115

INDEX

DRY AND LIQUID MEASUREMENT EQUIVALENTS

If you are converting the recipes in this book to metric measurements, use the following chart as a guide.

TEASPOONS	TABLESPOONS	CUPS	FLUID OUNCES
3 teaspoons	1 tablespoon		½ fluid ounce
6 teaspoons	2 tablespoons	⅛ cup	1 fluid ounce
8 teaspoons	2 tablespoons plus 2 teaspoons	⅙ cup	
12 teaspoons	4 tablespoons	¼ cup	2 fluid ounces
15 teaspoons	5 tablespoons	⅓ cup minus 1 teaspoon	
16 teaspoons	5 tablespoons plus 1 teaspoon	⅓ cup	
18 teaspoons	6 tablespoons	¼ cup plus 2 tablespoons	3 fluid ounces
24 teaspoons	8 tablespoons	½ cup	4 fluid ounces
30 teaspoons	10 tablespoons	½ cup plus 2 tablespoons	5 fluid ounces
32 teaspoons	10 tablespoons plus 2 teaspoons	⅔ cup	
36 teaspoons	12 tablespoons	¾ cup	6 fluid ounces
42 teaspoons	14 tablespoons	1 cup minus 2 tablespoons	7 fluid ounces
45 teaspoons	15 tablespoons	1 cup minus 1 tablespoon	
48 teaspoons	16 tablespoons	1 cup	8 fluid ounces

VOLUME	
¼ teaspoon	1 milliliter
½ teaspoon	2 milliliters
1 teaspoon	5 milliliters
1 tablespoon	15 milliliters
2 tablespoons	30 milliliters
3 tablespoons	45 milliliters
¼ cup	60 milliliters
⅓ cup	80 milliliters
½ cup	120 milliliters
⅔ cup	160 milliliters
¾ cup	175 milliliters
1 cup	240 milliliters
1 quart	950 milliliters

LENGTH		
1 inch	25	millimeters
1 inch	2.5	centimeters

WEIGHT	
1 ounce	30 grams
¼ pound	120 grams
½ pound	240 grams
1 pound	480 grams

OVEN TEMPERATURE			
250°F	120°C	400°F	200°C
275°F	140°C	425°F	220°C
300°F	150°C	450°F	230°C
325°F	160°C	475°F	250°C
350°F	180°C	500°F	260°C
375°F	190°C	525°F	270°C

Note: Measurement of less than ⅛ teaspoon is considered a dash or a pinch. Metric volume measurements are approximate.